WRITING
FOR
THE
MEDIA

PUBLIC RELATIONS AND THE PRESS

Sandra Pesmen

CRAIN BOOKS

740 Rush Street   Chicago, IL 60611

Published by Crain Books
A Division of Crain Communications, Inc.
740 Rush Street
Chicago, IL 60611

85 84 83 10 9 8 7 6 5 4 3 2 1

ISBN   0-87251-077-8
Library of Congress Catalog Card No. 82-072510

Printed in the United States of America

To Hal, Beth, and Curt, who have always been the real features in my life.

Contents

Exhibits

Acknowledgments

Grateful thanks to Crain Books Director Rich Hagle, who encouraged me to think this idea might work, and to Sheldon Liebman, Crain Books Editor, who kept marking these pages and turning them back until we got them right.

Introduction

When I was in college, I had one professor whose classes were always packed. Regardless of what he was teaching, students filled the seats, jammed the aisles, and even stood along the back wall of the classroom.

"How do you do it?" I once asked him. "Why do they pour in here to listen to you?"

And the late Dr. Paul Landis, professor of English literature at the University of Illinois, answered, "I've been around this campus long enough to learn what they want. They want information presented in a clear, simple, interesting way—so that's what I give them. Then I encourage them to go out and let others know what they're getting here."

With those few words, the man defined effective public relations, long before either of us knew what it was.

He also shared another important communications technique with me that day.

"When I give a lecture," he told me, "I always assume no one in my audience knows anything about my subject. I begin with basics and fill in every detail—so nobody feels left out, overwhelmed, or inadequate. In fact, the people who are familiar with my subject even puff up a bit and start to feel very good about knowing more than the others do, and that too keeps their attention."

So, with full credit to Dr. Landis, I'm going to do the same. I'll assume none of my readers knows anything about "writing for the media" or how basic journalism skills can be adapted for use in public relations work.

Of course, if you have been a public relations practitioner for a long time, you'll be familiar with some of the information in this book. In that case, lean back and enjoy your feeling of superiority. At the very least, however, you'll be reminded of a few things you've forgotten. And because *Writing for the Media* focuses on a particular area of public relations work, you'll probably encounter a number of ideas, strategies, and techniques you never heard before.

If you are new to public relations or have been away from it for a long time, you will undoubtedly find a good deal of useful advice and counsel that will help you launch or relaunch a successful public relations career. Because the field has changed substantially in recent years, both newcomers and returnees need an introduction to the most current information on media writing for public relations professionals.

The biggest change in the last decade has been the transformation of public relations from mongering to marketing. Let me explain.

In the 1950s and 1960s, the goal of many PR

types was simply to get their client's or company's name mentioned in the media. In pursuit of this goal, they acted as mere press agents, vaunting the company and its products through vague, untargeted, and carelessly written press releases and sometimes through flamboyant publicity stunts. They wined and dined reporters and sent lavish gifts to their media contacts in hopes of winning friends and influencing people in order to elicit a casual reference in the gossip columns.

Fortunately, that's all changed dramatically in the last ten years. Today, public relations is considered an integral part of the marketing function. As such, it requires extensive research, careful planning, and expert execution. Most successful public relations executives are respected professionals who are invaluable to organizations interested in using PR to sell goods and services and important to reporters who want accurate and credible information about both public and private companies—their products and services, their personnel, and their activities inside and outside the marketplace.

Whether you work in-house on a public relations staff or as an outside public relations counselor, you serve as a vital link between the media and your company or institution.

Today, every effective public relations specialist incorporates sophisticated marketing, promotional, and sales techniques in his work to develop and protect his clients' public images. If you hope to accomplish that, you must know how to write releases for the media in simple, clear newspaper style that will catch your reader's interest and explain important events succinctly and comprehensively.

It's one thing to understand the message your client wants to present, but unless you convey it to the media and convince reporters to write about it—you haven't helped anyone.

All publicists must master the basic news-writing skills in order to:

- Develop and write presentations to win accounts or put across new projects.

- Write daily business correspondence, company newsletters, in-house newspapers, and annual reports.

- Design and write clear, readable press kits that include a news release, a fact sheet, and a few story ideas that may be developed into newspaper or magazine features.

The goal of this book is to help you develop the writing ability to perform all three tasks and the know-how to put that ability to work in dealing with the press.

Throughout *Writing for the Media*, I have tried to provide as many examples as possible of both good and bad public relations writing. In addition, I have referred to the PR work of many companies, institutions, and public relations firms.

Most of the writing samples are from Chicago-based publications, and most of the references are to Chicago-area organizations. That's because I've worked closely with that city's top business people, PR executives, and journalists. After 25 years, I know them well and respect their abilities. And because the rules of the PR game are the same no matter where you play it, their work is representative of the best the business and journalism communities have to offer.

Sandra Pesmen

The PR Plan

Chapter 1

Finding the Image

Before you develop a public relations program for your client or company, you must determine exactly what you want to say. In order to make those decisions, you must have a clear definition of public relations.

Publicist Sheila King, president of her own firm and public relations instructor at Chicago's Roosevelt University, says, "Every client has an idea of the image he would like to have portrayed to the public. Every client also *has* a public image—a way in which he's viewed by the public.

"The function of a public relations consultant is to make sure the public image the client wants to have and the public image the client actually *does* have are one and the same."

For example, it's generally agreed that the following have specific and clear public images:

- IBM: A leader in the business machines field, so solidly dependable it's forgiven for the rumor that it makes salesmen sing company songs at corporate meetings.

- Sears, Roebuck: The store for mid-America, where shoppers feel they get the best deal because "Sears stands behind its own products."

- Hart Shaffner & Marx: Retail manufacturing giant, known for top-quality products, the first to open its own men's stores across the nation.

- McDonald's: The place to stop for a hamburger and a shake—and regardless of taste or cost, customers believe, "We do it all for you."

- Combined International: W. Clement Stone's Positive Mental Attitude has the public convinced the 61-year-old company will always be safe and successful, even after it merged with Ryan Insurance Group.

- International Harvester: Farm equipment manufacturing giant that fell to its knees in the 1980s downturn economy and seems unable to get up.

- Chrysler: Auto industry leader that's suffered serious setbacks from which it may not recover, despite Lee Iacocca's impressive TV campaign.

- Procter & Gamble: Maker of household and grocery products, with a reputation as pure as its Ivory soap—until the "satan curse" struck in 1982.

In some cases, such as IBM or Hart Shaffner & Marx, the public image and the desired image correspond. Therefore, the goal of the publicist is to sustain the public image—that is, to make sure the public continues to view the company the way it has in the past.

In other cases, such as Chrysler Corporation and International Harvester, the public image must be changed. The task of the public relations counselor is to change the company's public image so that it conforms to the company's desired image.

In still other cases, such as new companies—or established companies introducing a completely new line of products or services—the objective is to create a new image. Examples are the Aldi stores, which are trying to create the image of low overhead and low prices, and Philip Morris's Marlboro, which transformed a "woman's" cigarette into an image-enhancer for "macho" men.

The same would hold true for a company with a weak or vague public image.

There are four steps involved in this procedure:

1. *Research.* First, you must investigate the opinions, attitudes, and beliefs of people inside and outside the company. For example, in the case of a manufacturer, you must interview company personnel, including the sales staff that deals with both distributors and consumers. Then, you must find out what the public thinks—through interviews, surveys, and questionnaires. Once you've canvassed everyone's views, you must analyze the information you have collected. Then you must decide whether the actual image and the desired image of the company correspond. Besides gathering opinions to determine how the company would like to be seen by its various publics, you should also examine its products or services, marketing strategy, advertising, sales promotion, "position" in the market, research and development, and every other element that could conceivably contribute to the company's public image, including managerial style, corporate ac-

quisitions and growth, sales and profits, size and location of plant, and so on.

2. *Planning.* The next step is to report your findings to management. If the two images match, you should propose a "proactive" PR program that emphasizes the need to sustain the company's image and is designed to take advantage of public relations opportunities as they arise. If the two images don't jibe, you should develop a "reactive" PR program that stresses the need for change in the face of specific public relations problems. (Most PR proposals include both proactive and reactive elements.) Then you will work with the officers of the company to modify or expand the plan in order to adapt it to larger marketing goals and adjust it to budget limitations. Throughout this stage, you will be expected to present written explanations of and justifications for your proposals.

3. *Implementation.* Once your program has been approved, you must implement it by using every available means—that is, through speeches, letters, meetings, news releases, radio and TV spots, booklets, newsletters, bulletin board notices, billboards, etc. Remember, too, that every team has a captain who informs all the players of the game plan. As leader of the PR program, you must keep all the principals abreast of your progress—every step of the way. You must be able to explain your course of action to everyone who will be affected by it. The support of your colleagues is essential. The content of these communications should be "Here's what we're doing and why." Obviously, this step will require several more written reports.

4. *Evaluation.* It's to everyone's advantage to receive a clear statistical evaluation of the results of your program and the effectiveness of your techniques. This phase of the program can serve as a report card for you, for it shows what you accomplished on the job. Once again, it will demand a report written in a simple, clear, and interesting journalistic style.

EXERCISE 1-1

Below, list five well known people, places, or things that have favorable public images.

Below, list five people, places, or things with public images that should be changed.

Chapter 2

Planning the Program

In developing a public relations program, it is important to determine which "publics" you want to "relate" to. That is, you must find out who your audience is. Typically, companies have half-a-dozen or more different publics with whom they are interested in establishing and maintaining good relations. These include employees, stockholders, suppliers, distributors, members of the community, and consumers.

A flexible PR plan will address each of these groups on a regular basis. It will take advantage of every opportunity to publicize the company's desired image—thereby promoting its products or services and preventing public relations problems before they arise.

To this end, employees receive a weekly or monthly newsletter. Stockholders are sent an annual report and intermittent announcements. Suppliers and distributors are reached through trade magazines. Members of the community are invited to plant tours and offered the company's expert advice and special services through a speakers bureau and cooperative endeavors with community organizations, such as churches and schools.

Because consumers are the biggest and most important public, however, they should be com-municated with much more frequently—in fact, whenever anything that can be construed as "news" becomes available for public consumption. It is of great value to the company to pass on to actual and potential customers every bit of information that might enhance the company's public image. Possible topics include:

- New Products or services

- Changes in company policies

- Achievements, such as increased sales or profits, technological developments, plant openings or expansions, acquisitions, and large contract awards

- New promotions and advertising campaigns

- Special events

- Community and public service activities

- Executive activities, such as meetings, speeches, public appearances, travel, conference and convention sponsorship and participation

Of course, the more important the news, the more ambitious will be the public relations effort. While a brief news release sent to two local newspapers and a trade magazine might suffice for announcing a middle-management promotion, an elaborate press kit would be appropriate for publicizing a new product introduction or a company birthday-anniversary celebration.

In addition to these proactive, problem-preventing, opportunity-taking activities, an effective PR plan must also allow for more spontaneous, ad hoc responses to problems that arise unexpectedly and must be handled quickly but effectively. These reactive, problem-solving, remedial activities are needed to counteract *bad news*—negative reflections on the company's public image. They range from strikes to stockholder revolts, from actual or alleged problems with product quality and financial stability to FTC disputes and zoning law changes.

If the research conducted by the PR specialist has been thorough, some of these problems can be discovered before they become unmanageable and solved in the public relations program. Indeed, one of the advantages of a careful PR audit using both internal and external sources is that problems can be transformed into opportunities if they are spotted early and treated swiftly.

However, no PR plan can account for every contingency. The best that any publicist can do is watch for social, economic, and political trends and make the PR program flexible enough to handle the inevitable surprises offered by cranks, consumers, and competition.

Consider the problem facing Daniel Edelman, president of the international public relations firm that bears his name, in the early 1970s. At the time, the public was becoming very aware of ecology, and people were disturbed by large corporations that caused pollution.

"The Dial soap plant in Aurora, Ill., was emitting odors and there was some effluent going into the streams of the Fox River that runs through the state," Edelman remembers. "An irate citizen who named himself 'The Fox' started a personal campaign against the company.

"He plugged up our pipes, left signs around the area, wrote letters to the metropolitan and community newspapers, and generally won the sympathy and encouragement of the people in the area."

Since Daniel J. Edelman & Associates, Inc., had been handling public relations for Dial soap for a long time, it immediately took on the assignment of improving the company's image as a polluter.

"First we consulted with Dial about what could be done about improving the situation, and the corporation agreed to undertake a multi-million dollar program to accelerate technology and improve the plant productions. After several meetings with employees, we also decided to hold meetings with community leaders, to inform them of our progress."

A committee made up of corporate and community leaders was quickly established, and a slide show was prepared to run at Rotary and Kiwanis meetings and in the local schools. A series of news releases were sent to the local and metropolitan newspapers, and committee members from both the community and the company met with the news media to develop stories that would inform the public of the new improvements.

That public image problem was solved within six months.

Sometimes, however, a public relations campaign may prove to be an overreaction and a waste of time and money.

That was the case when a rumor began circulating in 1982 that Procter & Gamble was "in league with the devil" and the company's management became overly concerned about the effect of the rumor on P&G's reputation. It mounted a massive national publicity campaign and even sued some disc jockeys for allegedly spreading the rumor. It was a campaign *Advertising Age* claims was "perhaps unprecedented in scope in U.S. marketing" and largely unnecessary and ineffective in reaching people who might believe the rumors.

Actually, *Ad Age* surveys showed the principal effect of the campaign seemed to be to increase awareness of the rumor among people who were disinclined to believe the "devil worship" stories anyway.

Ad Age also suggested that although the costly public relations campaign may have been in itself harmless, "the whole affair does raise the question of whether the usually coolly analytic marketer overreacted to a rumor that all but a small minority of Americans seemed to dismiss on its face." When a company decides that mounting a public relations campaign is appropriate, however, the PR consultant has a large number of communications vehicles at his disposal. He can assist in writing letters to editors, aggrieved consumers, and community leaders. He can help company executives deliver speeches, sponsor meetings, and hold press conferences. He can offer tours, initiate community projects, and arrange special events.

Besides these person-to-person communications, the publicist also has access to a variety of print, broadcast, and visual media for dissemination of the public relations message. These include newspapers, magazines, radio, television, videotape and film, pamphlets, reports, newsletters, and outdoor displays.

By these means, the PR expert can keep all the publics with which a company is concerned fully informed of its plans, goals, and achievements. However, he or she must learn to use each medium to full advantage—which means knowing what to say, how to say it, and to whom to say it.

In order to encourage national and local print and broadcast media to take an interest in your company and help you spread the message of good will, your PR plan should eventuate in a complete press kit, which gives different media with different markets an opportunity to use materials addressed to their own particular audiences. Several stories can be written about a new product introduction, for example, including one about its marketing, another about its development, and yet another about its features and applications. The press kit should also contain profiles of company personnel and a fact sheet listing information about the product. Some feature story ideas should be included as well. Examples of these items are shown in Exhibits 2-1, 2-2, and 2-3.

EXHIBIT 2-1. The Profile.

FROM: Louise Palvig/Erica Preiss   *For Immediate Release*
          (312) 751-2121
FOR: James Joseph Cosmetics
          305 South Westmore
          Lombard, Ill. 60148

Biography of James Joseph

Thirty-year-old James Joseph has always had an innate sense of aesthetics and color. Born in Washington, D.C., James moved to New York City at an early age and, realizing his talents lay in the beauty field, began training at a hair salon in New York. He traveled to Europe in 1970, where he apprenticed at the Vidal Sassoon Salon on Bond Street in London.

James moved to Chicago in 1972, working at several prestigious Chicago salons on Oak Street and Michigan Avenue. He frequently served as makeup artist for television commercial productions and modeling photography assignments.

Frustrated with drab makeup foundations and uninteresting colors that were offered on the market, in 1975 James Joseph started research and development procedures for a new line of cosmetics. His wife Patricia—a model and hair and makeup specialist herself—aided him in the search for high-quality cosmetics. After six years of product testing at various New York manufacturing facilities, James began distributing cosmetics to Chicago area boutiques and salons.

Today, James has his own line of James Joseph cosmetics which are sold exclusively in major department stores. James believes his makeup is simple, yet elegant, providing a natural look for each individual and offering the necessary versatility to achieve even the most avant-garde look. He also believes in a highly trained staff and spends much of his time teaching his sales people about his products and about the fine art of applying makeup.

EXHIBIT 2-2. The Press Release.

FROM: Loiuse Palvig/Erica Preiss
(312) 751-2121
FOR: James Joseph Cosmetics
305 South Westmore
Lombard, Ill. 60148

For Immediate Release

JAMES JOSEPH COSMETICS TO BE OFFERED IN 24 STORES BY SPRING

James Joseph Cosmetics, Inc., a 2½-year-old Chicago cosmetics company, has introduced its full line to the major department store trade, announcing distribution through 24 leading outlets in the Chicagoland, Wisconsin, Houston and Dallas markets.

"The success of our line locally—evidenced by distribution figures which indicate James Joseph Cosmetics consistently has the highest volume stock turnover of any makeup line carried at department stores—encouraged us to pursue regional expansion," explains James Joseph, the 30-year-old cosmetics company entrepreneur.

James Joseph Cosmetics began its department store distribution in April, 1982, when the line was offered at four area Marshall Field & Company locations, including State Street/Chicago, Oakbrook Center/Oak Brook, Woodfield Mall/Schaumburg and Old Orchard Shopping Center/Skokie. By mid-September, seven additional Field's stores will carry the cosmetics at the following locations: Water Tower Place/Chicago, River Oaks/Calumet City, Hawthorne Center/Vernon Hills and Oak Park Mall/Oak Park in Illinois; the Mayfair Shopping Center/Wauwatosa, Wisconsin, and the Houston and Dallas outlets in Texas. Joseph anticipates his Marshall Field line will do close to $1 million worth of business by Fall, 1983.

"Our product sells well because it is suitable for anyone, young or old, conservative or au courant," says Joseph. "And, as we expand nationally, we know that we will find our products can sell in Boise, Idaho, as well New York City."

In addition to 11 Marshall Field locations, James Joseph products will also become available in early fall at four Wiebolt's department stores in the Chicago area—State Street/Chicago, Randhurst Shopping Center/Mt. Prospect, Ford City/Chicago and Harlem & Irving/Chicago. Sakowitz department store in Houston and Neiman-Marcus in Dallas will start carrying the line in early winter. And by Spring, 1983, the Bergner department store chain will add James Joseph Cosmetics.

James Joseph credits his success to dedicated research and product testing. A makeup artist who was unsatisfied with the drab colors he found in current products on the market, Joseph began development of his own cosmetics line six years ago. In early 1980, James Joseph Cosmetics became incorporated. Today, the complete cosmetics line features 25 vibrant-colored nail enamels, 20 lipsticks, eight lip glosses, 32 eye shadows, 12 blushes, four mascaras, six foundation bases, 12 eye and lip pencils and nine makeup brushes. The products' average retail price is $6.72.

"Some of my competitors charge three-and-a-half times what our products sell for," says Joseph, "and don't provide high-quality items or personalized counter service."

"We've spent countless hours perfecting these products. James Joseph nail polish doesn't chip, our mascara doesn't run, our shadows don't crease and our blushes stay on without fading. And with our product, you get a lot of color, not just a lot of powder."

A great deal of Joseph's time is spent training beauty consultants on the art of applying his makeup, as well as how to make a customer feel comfortable. "Our customers become long-term purchasers, not only because of our quality product, but our superior presentation and uncompromising service," he explains.

Joseph plans to serve the needs of his customers even further with the forthcoming introduction of a complete facial treatment line. Ten new items—including four or five moisturizers, undereye cream, astringent, skin freshener and eye makeup remover—will be unveiled by James Joseph in late 1982/1983.

James Joseph Cosmetics is headquartered at 305 South Westmore in Lombard, Ill. For further information, call (312) 627-4640.

Sept. 8, 1982

EXHIBIT 2-3. The Fact Sheet.

FROM: Louise Palvig/Erica Preiss
          (312) 751-2121
FOR: James Joseph Cosmetics
          305 South Westmore
          Lombard, Ill. 60148

For Immediate Release

JAMES JOSEPH COSMETICS
Fact Sheet

	Product	Average Retail Price
PRODUCT LINE:	25 Nail Enamels	$ 4.50
	20 Lipstick Shades	6.00
	8 Lip Gloss Shades	5.00
	32 Eye Shadow Colors	6.00
	12 Blush Colors	8.00
	4 Mascara Shades	7.00
	6 Foundation Bases	15.00
	12 Eye & Lip Pencils	6.00
	9 Makeup Brushes	4.00–10.00 each

Average Price: $6.72

FUTURE PRODUCT
   ADDITIONS: James Joseph Facial Treatment
                       Ten items, including moisturizers, under-eye cream, astringent, skin
                          freshener, eye makeup remover.

CURRENT STORE
   LOCATIONS: Marshall Field & Company—State Street,
                          Oakbrook, Old Orchard, Woodfield.

FUTURE STORE
   LOCATIONS: Marshall Field & Company—Water Tower,
                          River Oaks, Hawthorne and Oak Park Shopping Centers in Illinois;
                          Mayfair Center in Wisconsin; Houston and Dallas, Tex.

                       Wiebolt's—Randhurst, Ford City, State Street, Harlem & Irving.

                       Sakowitz—Houston, Tex.
                       Nieman-Marcus—Dallas, Tex.

                       Bergner's—Seven stores in northern and downstate Illinois, as well as
                          Wisconsin.

Sept. 8, 1982

EXERCISE 2-1

Earlier, you listed five people, places, or things that suffered from poor public images. Below, list ways in which you might change those images, as Edelman did for Dial soap.

EXERCISE 2-2

Assuming that your client or company agrees with your plan to improve its public image, your first step is to prepare a fact sheet about the company, such as the one prepared for James Joseph Cosmetics.

Prepare a fact sheet for your company below.

Chapter 3

Marketing the Message

When you've determined your public relations program, you're ready to begin writing public relations releases, informing the public of the image your client hopes to project.

But before you begin any communications project, you must find out whom you are writing to—and how you can best reach them.

The first step is to develop a demographic profile of your audience that tells you something about them. Be sure you know your potential readers'

- Sex
- Average age
- Professional or nonprofessional status
- Average income
- Educational level
- Lifestyle
- Workstyle
- Ethnic background
- Political and community involvement

Once you understand the people for whom you are writing and know what their interests are, the second step is to find out which publications are best for attracting their attention.

If you make the very common mistake of sending the same releases to all the media, with no concern as to who reads or watches what, the bulk of your work will end up in the editors' wastebaskets.

But once you know who reads which publication or tunes into what stations, you can focus each story so it will be of interest to specific audiences.

Let's examine an actual case.

Nick Nickolas, nationally known restaurateur, began his award-winning chain of Nick's Fishmarkets in Hawaii, then spread to Beverly Hills, opened a third in Chicago, and most recently expanded operations to Houston.

The audience that Nick wanted to attract is from 30 years old on up, both male and female, middle and upper executives, earning good salaries, living the fine life. They fly to vacations at least once a year, drink good Scotch, and are willing to spend lots of money to dine leisurely and graciously in Nick's elegant restaurants.

17

There are a variety of publications that help Nick's public relations counselor, Dan Roberts, get that message out to those potential diners—but each wants a different angle.

For example, people who read about Nick in *Esquire* magazine are interested in his high-flying personal lifestyle. They like learning that Nick has lived a Horatio Alger story. He began with nothing, worked as a bouncer in Hawaii, and now wears full-length mink coats.

They enjoy reading that Nick lives like an oil sheik in his Houston mansion and his Chicago lakefront condo, rides in a chauffered limo, and is escort to some of the country's most beautiful women.

Restaurant Hospitality magazine, on the other hand, is more interested in how Nick developed his unique Fishmarket concept. The story that magazine carried about Nick Nickolas included information about the equipment he's installed in his restaurants, the way he copes with restaurant critics, some new foods he features, and how he is the first restaurateur to ship some of them across the country daily, so he may offer them to his customers.

Also of interest to these readers is the way Nick has developed a "family" relationship with his partner, Jeff Harman, as well as with every one of his employees.

An entirely different story appeared in *Crain's Chicago Business*. That publication, an affiliate of Crain Communications, Inc., focused on what Nick invested in his Chicago operation, where he got those dollars, if the investment turned out to be as lucrative as he predicted it would be, and if the restaurant helped bring diners back to the Chicago Loop at night—as a boasting Nick also predicted it would.

Chicago business leaders who read that publication—and are potential customers—are interested in knowing Nick's marketing plans and profit projections.

A savvy public relations man like Dan Roberts makes sure he's familiar with all the publications that might be interested in stories relating to the several different facets of his unique client's business and personal life.

The best way to gain such insight is to start reading all the publications related to the field and to ask their advertising departments to send you the standard demographic kits most prepare for advertisers. Those kits will give you a picture of who the publication is promising to deliver to advertisers.

For example, the *Crain's Chicago Business* subscriber profile shows two pages of charts that reveal the following facts about the average reader:

- Median age, 45.5
- Sex, 89.6% male
- Education, 90.7% college
- Income $114,030, average household $100,850 average personal
- Management level, upper, 72.3% middle 23.2%

Too often, public relations counselors are not aware of the audience publications write for, and people in the media have to take them by the hand and lead them carefully to publications that are interested in their clients.

For example, a PR man from New York recently telephoned to tell me he had a client in his city who owned a large recruitment firm and who would be coming to Chicago to give a seminar. He thought it would be appropriate for *Crain's Chicago Business* to interview that person about how women who have finished rearing a family may begin plans to reenter the job market.

As you can see by the above demographics, *CCB*'s readers are 89% male, most are middle and upper executives, and they would not be particularly interested in such a story directed to housewives. Furthermore, the publication is strictly parochial. Regular readers know that if *CCB* is going to interview anyone about getting a job, it's going to be someone who is based in Chicago, handles Chicago clients, and gets jobs for them in Chicago companies. *The Chicago Tribune*, on the other hand, often runs stories about people in other cities because they are used on the *Tribune*'s national newswire.

Another big turnoff is the public relations person who clearly doesn't read the publications but calls up to try to plant a story anyway.

I had such a call recently. A PR woman phoned to say, "Hi, I don't read your paper, but I have a lot of restaurant accounts, and wouldn't it be nice to do a story about business breakfast meeting places?" If she had read the publication, she would have known that *CCB* did that story—a month before her telephone call.

Granted there are some publications that aren't very conscientious about determining readers' interests and simply "shoot buckshot" wherever the editors want to, sending frivolous stories out on their pages to anyone they happen to hit.

Amazingly—the very successful *Cosmopolitan* magazine is one of those.

In a column during the summer of 1981, Editor Helen Gurley Brown wrote:

> David [her husband] and I made a visit to Palo Alto, California, to visit David's alma mater, Stanford University. . . . I lectured to the journalism classes. . . . What a workout the children gave me! Several seemed upset because COSMO doesn't do any market research to 'find out what your readers want'. . . . I explained that good writing is our challenge . . . that our monthly sales checkup tells whether we're on target with subjects and, so far, our sales have gone straight up in sixteen years.

I'm afraid I'm inclined to agree with "the children" at Stanford University. It would be an excellent idea for *Cosmopolitan*—or any magazine—to conduct market research studies regularly. I submit that if someone examined the "sales checkup" more professionally, and determined how far "straight up" those sales have gone in 16 years and why that happened, the editors might be able to control editorial content more professionally, direct it more specifically to readers, and produce even larger profits.

It's also important for you to read regularly all of the publications you hope to crack and to know who writes each kind of story. Don't send real estate stories to the food editor, sports stories to the financial desk, or breaking news releases to an editorial assistant when the managing editor makes the decisions about whether or not to use those items.

One way to determine who's who is to keep track of bylines and the masthead of the publication, which usually lists editors by their area of specialization. Keep track of credits at the end of broadcasts in the same way for the same reason.

Also, check with secretaries, editorial assistants, and assistant producers to find out deadlines. There's nothing more frustrating to newspeople than getting a call from a publicist when they are on deadline. And there's no excuse for calling broadcasters when they're on the air. Everyone in the media has "quiet times" when they have finished their day's story, are scouting around for tomorrow's news—and welcome your help. That's the time to strike.

In addition to knowing everything there is to know about local publishers, broadcasters, national news publications, and trade journals, savvy PR people regularly read:

- *Editor & Publisher*
- *The Journalism Quarterly*
- *Nieman Reports*
- *The Columbia Journalism Review*

You should also have, on the shelf in your office:

- *Editor & Publisher Yearbook*
- *N. W. Ayer & Sons Directory of Newspapers and Periodicals*
- *National Directory of Newspapers*

A successful publicist also learns to use wire services and feature syndicates, weekly newspaper supplements, and a myriad of feature magazines, such as *Reader's Digest*, *Esquire*, and *Working Woman*, as well as specialty and trade publications, such as Gralla Publications' *Multi-Housing News* (for real estate) and Crain Communications's *Automotive News*.

You can also build a working list by using the resources of the *Ayer Directory*, *The Writer's Market*, and *Bacon's Publicity Checker*, published annually, and the directories of the Standard Rate and Data Service.

EXERCISE 3-1

List two of your clients or two corporations or prominent persons you would like to have as your clients.

Beneath each name, list three publications that would be interested enough in your client for you to approach them with a story idea.

Below, describe the story angle you would use to interest the editors of each of the different publications. Do the same for your local television and radio stations.

Part **II**

The News Release

Becoming a Reporter

Now that you have some idea of whom you're going to contact with your story ideas—and what angles you're going to suggest—you must learn how to gather enough information about your client to write a news release (or releases) to send to editors.

And the moment you reach this step, you've crossed over the line from publicist to reporter. Now, you have to pick up your pencil, get a notebook, ask questions, and jot down answers. Then, you go back to the office and write a news story.

Welcome to the club.

Recently, I served on a panel with the editor of a travel magazine and the editor of a national advertising trade publication. I listened with growing discomfort, while both women insisted they liked their jobs, "even though I don't work on a daily metropolitan newspaper."

Both stressed the advantages of their positions. Defensively, both said they enjoyed higher salaries, advanced faster, and traveled more than they would have on a daily paper.

But it seemed to me that both women protested far too much.

I've had a lot of reporting jobs since I graduated from journalism school many years ago, determined to make my living as a writer.

I've worked for a large metropolitan daily newspaper, a small metropolitan news service, a small town daily, weekly community papers, business publications, and a magazine.

During the five years I chose to retire and rear two children, I worked as unpaid editor of a newsletter for the League of Women Voters and volunteered to edit the monthly publication put out by our school district's PTA.

Never during any of that time did I ever make excuses for my work—as my colleagues on the panel seemed to be doing at that seminar. As far as I'm concerned, all editorial work is equally satisfying. No matter where I ply my craft, I try to do the same quality of work, striving for excellence in exactly the same way. In each case, I found, the satisfaction that came from seeing the final printed product was always fulfilling.

I define journalists as all people who go out to do a story—regardless of whom they're writing for.

They thoroughly investigate the subject, take to the streets and interview as many people as possible, study the information they have gathered, outline it, think about it, and talk about it. Then, they begin to put it together in an orderly fashion, placing the most important facts first. Finally, they transform the facts into a clear, simple, and interesting story.

Anyone who does that for a living qualifies as a reporter in my book.

So, as you get ready to collect the facts about your clients, remember you're going to be a reporter too—and good journalism is nothing more than good thinking. It means finding the right information, even if you have to take charge of the interview and guide your subject back to your questions now and then. It means organizing your facts, once you have them, and writing them clearly. If you can do that, you're a professional journalist, and you'll never have to make excuses for your work.

Granted, not all of us can turn out journalism on the level of syndicated columnists like Ellen Goodman, Mike Royko, and Jimmy Breslin. But we can all learn to be fairly good craftsmen. And, if we follow simple directions, we should all be able to produce readable stories that quickly tell the reader what he or she needs to know.

Unfortunately, there are too many people functioning in the public relations capacity who don't know how to write a release that accomplishes those goals. Common mistakes to watch out for are wordiness, puffery, and poor organization.

Recently the *Wall Street Journal* printed a story about a survey conducted by Brouillard Communications, a division of J. Walter Thompson Co., New York, showing that business editors at daily newspapers wade through stacks of corporate news releases every day, and most of those editors find fault with much of what they see.

The survey was taken among 206 business and financial editors of daily papers throughout the country. The 111 editors who responded said the most common fault was that releases lacked local relevance and significance.

One business editor of a California paper said, "Very few have a local angle. Many are about companies thousands of miles away."

Nearly six in every ten editors cited "irrelevant management commentary," and more than half complained that "important information is buried." Nearly half cited poor writing as a common flaw, and others complained that often information in the releases is not complete, the contact person at the company isn't listed or is difficult to reach, and the releases are too wordy, boring, and superficial.

Examples of the latter are shown in Exhibits 4-1 and 4-2.

EXHIBIT 4-1. News Release: Ambience Isn't Everything.

The Garden of Reinhard Barthel's Tower Garden and Restaurant, 9925 Grosse Point Rd., Skokie, is one of the loveliest outdoor dining spots in the Chicago area. Colorful umbrellas shade round tables. Evergreens and oaks provide natural shade, giving an ambience of a true country garden spot.

Luncheon and dinner are served in the Garden during good weather Monday through Friday, 11:30 A.M. to 10:30 P.M., and on Saturday, 11:30 A.M. to 11:30 P.M. The restaurant is closed on Sunday.

All major credit cards are accepted and there is a plentitude of parking.

EXHIBIT 4-2. News Release: A Plentitude of Platitudes.

Earth Angel: A Substantial New Spirit From Designer Spiros Zakas

While Earth Angel is designer Spiros Zakas' first venture into an active partnership in an operation which he designed, his talent has greatly enriched Chicago's dining-out scene in recent years.

Designer of the Pump Room; Ambria; Bastille; Toulouse and the late, lamented Le Rendezvous (as well as at least eight others in the Chicago area), Zakas has brought restaurant design to sophisticated levels not encountered here before.

While they are always elegant, they are also constantly evocative of special places in time and space. The Pump Room is a superb example of English Regency reworked into relevance to our own era. Ambria is understated Art Nouveau. Toulouse is warmly and sensuously contemporary. Bastille is the quintessence of the countryside of France.

Earth Angel—Just a Place in Time—evokes an era just as decidedly, but the design concept has at its heart relevance to the moods of today's patrons. There is nothing rigid . . . just a gentle evocation of a period more mellow than now, a period whose time has certainly come again.

The mellow-mooded period is evoked through not only the decor, but the imaginative selection of recorded music "broadcast" from the DJ booth as well as the recorded video elements from an earlier era shown on monitors throughout Earth Angel.

Zakas opened Earth Angel in Chicago because he loves the City and the receptive attitude it has always shown to his work. Soon, however, Earth Angels will be alighting all around the U.S. We'll let you know more about that as the concept moves on out.

Both news releases are clearly superficial. They don't tell us anything newsworthy about the restaurants. The first says a few words about ambience, and the second—a "mood" piece—goes on and on about the same subject but somehow manages to say even less in more space. Curiously, neither one says anything at all about the main business of restaurants—food and drink.

One editor responding to the public relations survey also cited timeliness as a problem. He pointed out that many releases arrive after the event. "By that time," he said, "it's wastebasket material."

EXERCISE 4-1

Rewrite the following wordy release into a short, informative two-paragraph story that tells the restaurant's plans simply and clearly.

On the Fourth of July weekend (Saturday and Sunday), Chef Lucien will toast the American Independence Day with champagne for all diners. A free bottle of delicious, chilled Korbel champagne will be served with dessert at every table for four. And L'Escargot's regular menu with its wide range or appetizers and entrees will be enhanced with a special red/white/blue(berry) dessert. The restaurant will be open from 5:00 until 10:30 p.m. on Saturday, July 4th. On Sunday, July 5th, L'Escargot's famous brunch will be served from 11:30 a.m. until 2:30 p.m., with dinner service from 5:30 until 10:30 p.m. Free champagne will be served at both meals on Sunday. On the Fourth of July weekend, L'Escargot salutes quality American vineyards by featuring two American house wines: Heitz Cellars Chablis (white) and Fetzer Zinfandel (red).

Bastille Day, July 14, celebrates that fall of the French Bastille in 1789. Bastille Day will be observed at L'Escargot with candlelight dinners Friday and Saturday (July 10 and 11) where diners can choose from the regular menu (ranging from $16.50 to $19.50) and enjoy a special Bastille Day dessert. On Sunday, July 12, the $11.50 Bastille Day brunch will whet appetites with such appetizer selections as cold monkfish on eggplant, and omelette Tonkinoise, Chef Lucien's French version of egg foo yong. The official Bastille Day menu is too mouthwatering to describe, so it is attached to this information piece. Suffice it to say, diners at L'Escargot on Sunday, Monday and Tuesday, July 12, 13 and 14, can choose from the six course special Bastille Day dinner menu at a fixed price of $21.50.

Chapter 5

Presenting the Facts

Although you may be a very talented writer, you may never publish stories, books, or articles. It's easier to live with that fact if you know you may use your writing skills and talent in a variety of other satisfying ways. You may send responsible, well-written news stories out of your typewriter, thereby making a significant contribution to the company for which you work.

In fact, I often think that understanding our limitations—and coming to terms with them—frees us to use our skills in a more productive way. Once we admit we're never going to win a Pulitzer Prize, we can relax and enjoy doing what we do well with great satisfaction and a whole lot less frustration.

And that brings us to the difference between literature and journalism. Over the years, students have repeatedly asked me what that is, and it took a while before I figured out the answer.

Finally, I decided that literature is using your imagination to dream up a story—setting and characters—then taking your time to polish it up until it becomes a finished work of art.

Another major characteristic of literature—i.e., poetry, drama, essays, novels, and short stories—is that its writers usually start with specific details and work toward a general message and tell their tales in chronological order.

Journalism, on the other hand, involves walking out into the street to get your whole story—plot, characters, setting, everything—then speeding back to the office, writing it against the ticking clock, and rushing it into print or onto an editor's desk.

In other words, when we write news, the story is out there waiting for us, and our job is to present it without changing the facts.

Even if newswriting is not as creative as writing a novel, the immediacy of it often makes it more exciting and lends a sense of adventure that cannot be found in any other line of work.

Newswriters perform their task by using a form they call the inverted pyramid. They crowd as much of the important message as possible into the first paragraph and then add less pertinent facts, according to importance, as the story continues. The least necessary portion comes at the bottom, where it may be clipped off for lack of space.

Journalists long ago discovered that the best way to create an "inverted pyramid story" is to make sure the first few sentences, which they call the "lead," contain "the five Ws and an H," which are Who, What, Why, When, Where, and How.

The purpose of doing that is to get all the relevant information to the reader quickly—in order to make reading easier, to satisfy curiosity, and to make headline writing and page make-up easier.

Below is an excellent example, taken from a daily newspaper, that shows how the five Ws are arranged at the top of the story.

The headline reads: "Ex-Busboy found guilty in Hilton Fire."

The story begins: "Philip Cline, a former busboy, was found guilty Friday of murder and arson for starting last February's blaze at the Las Vegas Hilton that killed 8 persons and injured 200."

That sentence completely summarizes what the story has to tell. The reporter continues for 100 words to give the reader more details of the incident and the events that led up to it. But the first line follows the first rule of journalism: It gives the reader the five Ws right away.

The same professional style is obvious in the news release prepared by Public Relations Counselor Daniel F. Roberts of Chicago (Exhibit 5-1). We've drawn in the inverted pyramids that reveal its form.

In this release, the reader grasps immediately who is doing what, when, where, and why. Roberts has even wisely chosen the "who" as the lead item because Dr. Reeder is a celebrity, particularly among students of Russian culture, who would be most likely to attend. However, the release could have featured the talk instead of the speaker.

In that case, the story would have begun:

> "Boris Anisfeld in the World of Art: Paintings and Theatre Design" will be discussed by Russian culture authority Dr. Roberta Reeder at 2 P.M. Saturday, Jan. 23, at Gilman Galleries, 277 E. Ontario St., where a major retrospective of the late artist's works currently is on display.

The rest of the information would be presented the same way, and in both cases the least important facts would be at the bottom, to be clipped off if space problems demanded it.

Unfortunately, there are a lot of reporters and public relations counselors who can't come to terms with the simplicity of journalism. Many PR people, for example, keep sending out news releases that take entirely too long to read because they are too literary, too imaginative, and too complicated.

Granted, some of them are tributes to their authors' literary virtuosity. But it would be a great kindness if the writers didn't clutter up editors' business day with that kind of mail.

The news release presented in Exhibit 5-2, for example, offers the media no real news. It is simply an essay-writing exercise for the author. It's possible that the client was naive enough to consider it part of an image building process. But, in fact, it created a poor impression of the company that approved it and encouraged the writer to make a habit of sending out "no news" releases.

A lead telling us that Chicago has always been notorious for Arctic winters, and that Carole Dorsch, Elizabeth Arden Salon manager, suggests women put more cream on their faces before going outside isn't likely to stop the presses. Few editors would get to the astonishing finish about the use of goose grease in Siberia. If they did, however, most would be unable to resist putting a question mark in place of the exclamation marks before throwing the release away. This news release, carefully sent to beauty and fashion editors, might work, however, if it began with the important facts:

> Two Elizabeth Arden moisturizers, "Visible Difference" and "8-hour Cream," will help both men and women cope with the damage extremely cold weather does to the skin, according to Carole Dorsch, manager of Elizabeth Arden Salon, 717 N. Michigan Ave.

On the positive side, publicist Cynthia Raskin, of Ruth Rashman & Associates Public Relations, handles the sixth annual Christmas Show and Sale at her client's ceramic studios in a

EXHIBIT 5-1. The Inverted Pyramid Form.

FOR IMMEDIATE RELEASE

CHICAGO (Jan. 8, 1982)—Dr. Roberta Reeder, noted author and speaker on Russian culture, will present a free slide lecture on Boris Anisfeld at 2 P.M. on Saturday, Jan. 23, at Gilman Galleries, 277 E. Ontario St., where a major retrospective of the late artist's works currently is on display.

Titled "Boris Anisfeld in the World of Art: Paintings and Theatre Design," the talk by Dr. Reeder—a visiting fellow at Harvard University's Russian Research Center—will highlight the artist's work in relation to those of his contemporaries in the fields of art, music and dance in Russia during the early 1900s. This group includes composers Stravinsky and Prokofiev, artists Bakst and Benois and ballet producer Diaghilev.

Anisfeld later immigrated to the U.S. and became head of the advanced painting department at the School of the Art Institute of Chicago—a post he held for 30 years.

Dr. Reeder's talk is open to the public; no reservations are required. For further information, call 337-6262.

For further information, contact:
Dan Roberts at (312) 951-1020

EXHIBIT 5-2. A "No News" News Release.

WINTER SKINCARE TIPS FROM ELIZABETH ARDEN

Chicago has always been notorious for arctic winters and this year particularly cold temperatures down to −26°F and wind chill factors of −80°F leaves skin dry and chapped.

"Always be sure to put more cream on your face and any parts of the body that will be exposed before going outside," recommends Carole Dorsch, Elizabeth Arden Salon Manager. "Exposed skin is always vulnerable to the wind and cold, but the entire body is affected by dryness and penetrating cold. Putting on more lotion before wearing gloves or mittens provides some extra warmth and helps prevent uncomfortable chapping." Carole suggests that both men and women use Elizabeth Arden's "Visible Difference" moisturizers for face and body. "Visible Difference" is absorbed by the skin through 21 cell layers and works with the body's natural chemicals to soften and protect the skin.

Another product recommended by Elizabeth Arden skincare experts is their "8-Hour Cream," a moisturizer that lasts all day or night. Carry a small bottle of cream or lotion in your purse or briefcase and apply during the day as necessary. Call or stop by the Elizabeth Arden Salon, 717 N. Michigan Ave., 266-5750, to pick up your favorite lotion and talk to a skincare expert about winter skin problems.

Rumor has it that in Siberia people use goose grease to soften and protect their skin . . . Aren't you glad that we have Elizabeth Arden!!!

professional manner in the release shown in Exhibit 5-3.

The lead sentence explains simply and exactly what is going to happen, and it includes all five Ws at the top. Raskin follows the inverted pyramid form, adding less important facts as the release continues. She includes a description of the sale items, provides other important information, and finishes with a helpful telephone number.

EXHIBIT 5-3. A Good News Release.

FOR IMMEDIATE RELEASE

FROM: Lill Street Studios   CONTACT: Cynthia Raskin
       1021 West Lill Street   Ruth Rashman
       Chicago, illinois 60614   467-7142

CLAY CABARET

Lill Street Studios, 1021 West Lill Street, will hold its 6th Annual Christmas Show and Sale, Saturday, December 5 (10 AM—6 PM) and Sunday, December 6 (noon—6 PM). There is no charge for the ceramic celebration where the work of the studio's 16 cooperative artists will be on sale. Spiced cider and popcorn will be on tap. Sale continues through December 31.

Lill Street is unique in that the public may watch the spectrum of the whole clay process—from the raw material to the finished product. The public may watch the clay being manufactured and where the work is made. Artists will be on hand for demonstrations and commissions. On exhibit will be the largest selection of pottery in the midwest. All this takes place in the 100-year-old multi-storied converted CTA Horse Barn in which Lill Street is housed.

Wares range from culinary cookware ($20 and under) and household items (flower arrangers, candle stick holders, trivets, soap dishes) to sculptural work ($100 and over) and miniature clay houses ($350 and up).

Lill Street Studios has a gallery open to the public through the holidays (Monday through Friday 9—5, Thursday 9—8, Saturday 10—5, Sunday noon—5), offers classes for all ages and levels, and gives tours for schools, art groups and other interested parties. Call 477-0701 for more information.

FYI: ALL MEDIA ARE INVITED TO LILL STREET'S PREVIEW PARTY, FRIDAY, DEC. 4, 5—10 PM (CHAMPAGNE, JEROME'S BAKERY COOKIES, MUSIC BY ARS NOVA ENSEMBLE).

EXERCISE 5-1

Below is an excellent news release about a soccer clinic to be presented at the National Sports & Fitness Expo in Chicago. Read it carefully. Then, write an analysis of why you believe it is effective. If you have any criticisms, add those too.

NATIONAL SPORTS & FITNESS EXPO PRESENTS SOCCER CLINIC SPONSORED BY THE CHICAGO STING, MARCH 27

The Chicago Sting, 1981 North American Soccer League Champs, will sponsor free soccer clinics at the National Sports & Fitness Expo, Saturday, March 27 beginning at 10:15 A.M., at the O'Hare Expo Center in Rosemont, Ill. The day-long event will include two clinics, one for coaches and one for young soccer players, both conducted by Al Miller, one of the winning-est coaches in the NASL. In addition, popular team mascot "Stanley Sting" will be on hand.

The day begins at 10:15 A.M. with the Youth Coaches Clinic. Miller will lecture on the techniques and strategies of effective coaching from 10:15 A.M. until noon. From noon until 1:15 P.M., a participation clinic will be held for the coaches. The first 200 coaches to sign up or come to the soccer clinic will receive a complimentary ticket to the Chicago Sting vs. New York Cosmos game.

From 2:30 until 5:30 P.M., a Youth Players Clinic will be conducted by Miller for soccer players from 6 to 15 years of age. This skill assessment and instructional clinic will award the first 300 kids to participate with a free ticket to the Sting vs. Cosmos game, as well.

Miller has become known throughout the U.S. as one of the leading authorities on youth soccer coaching.

EXERCISE 5-2

Read the following release from the American Medical Association carefully. Then rewrite it simply and concisely.

Select Safe Toys For Kids' Christmas

Santa Claus is coming soon. And that means that Dad and Mother are out doing the shopping for the toys that old St. Nick will leave under the tree for the youngsters of the family.

Toys—all the way from a rubber ball to a shiny new bike—are a part of growing up. The child without a toy or two—or two dozen—at Christmas is a forlorn tot indeed.

The chances are that your youngsters will open their gifts Christmas morning and have a large time getting acquainted with their new toys. But in all too many households across the nation the toys themselves will dim the happy Christmas season by causing accidents and injuries.

The American Medical Association offers some simple tips for selecting toys that will help insure a completely happy Christmas—

- Beware of small toys that can be swallowed, flammable toys, and toys with rough or sharp edges.

- All electric toys should be safe. Look for the safety approval label on the cord and on the toy itself.

- Avoid toys made of lead or colored with lead-based paints. You're unlikzly to encounter these today, as the dangers of lead poisoning are well known. But it's wise to be safe.

- Baby's toys should be too large to put in the mouth, washable, light-weight and non-brittle.

Eye injuries are a particular hazard from Christmas toys. Slingshots, air rifles, archery sets and even the spring-action toy pistols that propel sticks capped with rubber cups have caused eye injuries.

The air rifle, or B-B gun, is still a threat, even though its use is forbidden in many communities. If you give your child an air rifle, impress upon him the danger of the ricochet. Many air rifle injuries come from the small shot bouncing off a fence post or the side of a house. A target backed with a bag of sand or straw is a must for air rifle marksmen.

Christmas tree ornaments, particularly the strings of small lights, are potential hazards. Some of the brands of tree lights are flimsily wired and can be fire hazards. Old and frayed light strings are dangerous. Discard them.

Handle ornaments and lights with care. Keep the extra bulbs and the discarded bulbs out of the reach of the tots.

Chapter 6

Developing the Lead

Now, it's time to pick up the hefty pack of information you've gathered from newspaper clippings, interviews, library research, and annual reports, and prepare to write major news stories, as opposed to short announcements, about your client.

Begin to read and reread your materials. Then read it all again. Immerse yourself in every fact and facet of your subject that you can put your hands on. Memorize it in any order. Just let it seep into your brain and burrow into the corners. Those facts will pop out when you need them later.

While you're going over your notes, take out a set of colored pencils. This is a useful method for "organizing" a story.

If, for example, you've interviewed the president of a corporation about his company's sudden increase in revenues, begin marking everything the man said about the financial background of the company in red pencil. Use blue to underline any remarks he made about the principals of the company. Use green to underline any comments he made about the founders. Take out the orange pencil and use it to mark portions of your notes that deal with restructuring plans, and use yellow to underline com-

ments about where the company hopes to be in 15 years. Use the black pencil to draw lines under new plans for expansion and marketing.

This color coding will do two things. First it will put your notes in some kind of order, because no matter how well you lead your subject, he probably won't talk in outline form. Second, this method will help you commit the facts to memory.

Next, make a list of the four most important things you want to tell about the topic. Consider why you are bothering to write this story at all. What lasting impressions are you trying to make?

After considering all of that, and considering who your reader is and what he or she needs to know—you come to the most difficult and challenging part of any news writing assignment: finding the lead.

You won't be the first reporter to spend sleepless nights trying to do that.

There's a true story still told in the Chicago journalism community about the young, beautiful Ivy League English major who swept into a daily newspaper office in that city wearing a full-length mink coat. She was hired by the promotions department to sit at O'Hare Field and do short interviews of celebrities as they hopped on and off planes. Some editor in the front office thought the feature would increase circulation.

Unfortunately, the project, badly conceived and poorly executed, was stopped after only a few months. But that left the newspaper stuck with an unnecessary member of the Chicago Newspaper Guild that it couldn't fire. Not knowing what else to do with this witty young beauty, the editors plopped her into the financial department, where they hoped she would learn the profession by writing short news items.

The poor thing sat there for a week with one story. Then, finally, shaking her head, she turned to the man next to her and said, "You know what? I think writing the first paragraph is the hard part."

Don't laugh. I know some publicists who still feel that way, as you can see by the release in Exhibit 6-1.

Even if the writer conducted a very poor interview and came away with a poverty of ideas, there had to be something more newsworthy than "Ladies, are you looking for an exciting evening of entertainment?"

So how do you find the lead?

I like to think of the lead as my entrance into a story. It's like the Statue of Liberty in that it's the first thing strangers see as they come this way; it catches their attention and makes them want to stay.

Keep in mind that the lead you choose in the beginning may not stay with the story to the end. Sometimes, when you come back and read the story later, you'll find another fact further down that you think is more important. You're free to change it. On other occasions, the editor who reads the story after you turn it in may find something else he or she thinks is more important and will change it.

There's never a way to prove who's right and who's wrong. It's simply a matter of opinion, and if you're both putting aside your egos, you will probably come up with the best lead for the story.

You begin to find the lead after you have studied your notes, underlined with colored pencils, and thought about the facts for a while.

Next, I always try to find someone who'll listen to me a few moments. I force a friend, family member, fellow reporter, or editor to ask me, "What's the story about?"

Since the listener is usually hopping from one foot to the other—impatient to flee—I have to give the answer in one or two sentences. I find it's usually a pretty decent lead.

Another method I employ is to sit down, put paper into the typewriter and begin, "Dear Aunt Rose, Guess what I learned today?" The next paragraph, usually consisting of one or two sentences, is generally a workable lead.

I've given that suggestion to so many of my students at Northwestern University's Evening Division in the last ten years, I think there must now be reporters all over the country who sit down at their visual display terminals, sign on, and begin their stories with "Dear Aunt Sandy."

Another method is the one suggested to a new reporter one afternoon many years ago by Richard Christiansen, syndicated critic-at-large of the *Chicago Tribune*.

Dick turned to the nervous writer, who was twisting her hands and ready to cry, and said, "Now stop worrying. Just sit down at your desk and start typing. Pretty soon it'll pop up."

How will you recognize the lead when you think of it, hear it, or see it? The crux of the whole matter is: *The lead makes a promise your story fulfills.*

That isn't to say that it's simple to write a lead or learn the knack of finding one. All journalists write and rewrite leads, sometimes as they're chasing their stories all the way to the copy desk.

One of the things that makes it so hard to find a lead is that newswriting is rarely done in chronological order. You sometimes have to go to the end of your notes to find the beginning of your story.

In journalism circles, professionals like to tell the tale about the new reporter who covered his first meeting at city hall and then returned to the newsroom to write this story:

At 7 P.M. Tuesday in City Hall Mayor John A. Smith called the meeting to order. The secretary read the minutes of the last

EXHIBIT 6-1. The First Paragraph Is the Hardest.

"LADIES NIGHT OUT" EVENING
MAY 12 AT CINDERELLA ROCKEFELLA

Ladies, are you looking for an exciting evening of entertainment for you and your friends? Well, Peter Adonis' Traveling Fantasy Show will be offering an evening of entertainment and much more at Cinderella Rockefella on *Tues., May 12 beginning at 8* P.M. This "Ladies Night Out," featuring two hours of all-male burlesque and comedy, will be held for one night only with a $5 per person admission for the show. Tickets will be available at the door on a first-come basis. Cinderella Rockefella is located adjacent to the Arlington Park Hilton at Euclid Rd. in Arlington Heights, Ill. Men are invited to Cinderella Rockefella following the "Ladies Night Out" program with the club open until 2 A.M. for this special event of entertainment.

The Peter Adonis' Traveling Fantasy Show is no ordinary nightclub act. Designed for female audiences, women are invited to relax and enjoy as five male dancers engage in healthy, old-fashioned burlesque—of a new and different kind! For the past two years, the "Ladies Night Out" show has performed every night of the month, thrilling female audiences across the country. The show is not vulgar or rude, says Bob Gregory who serves as emcee. "Our show is pure class," he adds.

Cinderella Rockefella offers music enthusiasts an ideal setting for experiencing both live and recorded entertainment. The sound and lighting system, designed by Juliana's Sound Services of London, is electronically controlled by one of today's most advanced computers and offers outstanding musical clarity throughout this $3.2 million facility. For further information on the special "Ladies Night Out" show, please call 394-2000.

meeting, which was held two weeks ago.

The aldermen approved two variations of the zoning ordinance and the installation of three new stop lights downtown was approved.

At 9:15 P.M. the secretary shot the mayor.

When trying to determine your lead, think about which of the five Ws is the most important.

The *who* will be most important when you announce a promotion, appointment, or staff expansion:

Thomas J. Even has been appointed senior vice president/marketing of Smith Creative Advertising Agency.

The *what* will be most important when you announce a new addition:

The $4 million lower level of the Happy Day Hotel opened today, showing off its three ballrooms and two conference rooms, all equipped with complete video televiewing equipment—the first in this city.

The *why* is most important when the effect of the news will have an impact on the reader:

In order to save riders of public transportation another fare hike, the mayor has dumped a large portion of his campaign warchest into the transportation department's budget.

The *where* is important if the location is in the news:

Newly bankrupt Goldblatt's store, right on the State Street Mall, is to be the site of the city's new Central Branch Library.

The *when* can't be overlooked if it makes your story more dramatic:

Shortly after midnight, two masked gunmen broke into the Standard Station at Madison Ave. at Clark St., terrorized two employees, tied them up, and left, taking $50 in cash.

The *how* goes first in most action stories:

Ron LeFlore was off with the crack of the bat as if he were a sprinter responding to the starter's pistol. By the time the ball came down near the wall in left center, the new center fielder for the White Sox was camped under it.

In Exercises 6-1 through 6-5, write news stories using the leads suggested and based on the facts provided.

EXERCISE 6-1

Try a "Who" lead here:

> Highland Park, Ill., has just appointed a new Park District director. The Park board president, Ralph Cianchetta, announced the appointment. It will be effective February 1.
>
> The new director is Connie Skibbe, 30, who replaced Ernie Nance, who resigned to become assistant director of parks and recreation in Dallas.
>
> Ms. Skibbe is the first woman ever appointed to head a park district in Illinois. She was formerly the district's superintendent of recreation. She has a degree in park and recreation administration from the University of Illinois and has worked in Highland Park nine years.

EXERCISE 6-2

Write this story with a "When" lead.

Jerome S. Leavitt, chairman, and Arnold K. Leavitt, president of Union Liquor Company, made an announcement Tuesday.

The pair named a new sales manager in charge of the newly formed hotel and restaurant division. He is Arthur B. Siegel, who will be joining the company on February 1, 1982. Siegel started in the liquor business in the fall of 1937. Most of that time has been spent with Gold Seal, a large wholesaler.

EXERCISE 6-3

This story would be a natural for a "Why" lead:

> Miles Davis, legendary jazz trumpeter, had been planning to present a concert on January 29–30. It was to be in Niles's Mill Run Theater.
>
> That engagement has been canceled because Davis is hospitalized, but persons holding tickets for either date can refund them at original point of purchase. For information call 298-2170.

EXERCISE 6-4

Do this one using a "Where" lead, since the place referred to is so special:

> Alper Richman Salon is going to begin giving fur fashion shows each Wednesday afternoon. All the newest furs, from lynx and sable to black willow mink, coyote, and fox will be shown, while commentary is given on each design, and models walk to piano accompaniment.
>
> The shows will be held in the elegant Palm Court of the Drake Hotel during tea time, from 4:00 P.M. to 5:00 P.M.

EXERCISE 6-5

"What" seems to be the most important of the five Ws here:

>The Illinois Humanities Council will meet Thursday, January 14, according to director Robert Klaus. The meeting will be at the Westin Hotel in Chicago.
>
>The Council will consider 37 grant proposals from community organizations throughout the state. Twenty-two of them are designed to strengthen humanities education in public secondary schools.

Chapter 7

Learning the Basics

Now that you understand the difference between journalism and poetry, you're ready to expand on what I call the "shoemaking" skills necessary to produce legible, timely, well-organized news stories and releases.

Keep in mind the fact that the style of the news story is different from that of an expository essay. The news story has a special, clean look because it has simple, short sentences with short, simple words and paragraphs shorter than they would be in an English class theme. We break some rules to keep sentences to an average of ten words and paragraphs to two or three sentences. The idea here is the K.I.S. principle: Keep It Simple. The simple style tends to allow more white space on the page, which is inviting to the reader. It's also easier to read on a moving bus or train than long, gray stories that make the reader squint and strain.

These rules, long adhered to by newspaper people, were set forth years ago by Rudolf Flesch in his book *The Art of Plain Talk*. He advocated only a 17-word sentence average and advised strongly against more than 37 words with affixes in each 100 words.

His formula also claimed that the more personal a piece of writing is, the greater its readability is. He advocated the use of verbs and warned against too many prepositions, conjunctions, and adverbs, which he called "empty words."

In the beginning, it's difficult to follow Flesch's rules, especially when you're trying to write fact-filled sentences. The biggest problem for most beginners is trying to pack too much into one sentence—in an effort to get all five Ws and H in at once.

But once you get the hang of it, you'll be able to send the news along in a series of short, clear sentences—in a rat-tat-tat effect—instead of a few long, boring sentences. You simply have to take the time to practice and develop the habit.

Here are some general rules:

- Keep sentences short. Break up long sentences into two, taking out the connecting word.

- Don't use important or unusual words more than once in each paragraph.

- Don't use an important or unusual word twice in the same sentence or repeat it too soon in the same paragraph.

- Don't begin a sentence with the same word with which the preceding sentence ended.

- Don't begin anything with "There will be."

- Glance over your finished story and make sure two succeeding paragraphs don't begin with the same word.

- Remember to cut out redundancy, words that repeat each other. (The preceding sentence is a perfect example.)

- When you've finished a story go back and strike out as many words as you can.

Unnecessary words bore the reader, take up his precious time, and cost the publisher money for printing. Your mission is to present the lean, bare facts, so edit out superfluous words. Then, when you think you've done that, go back and brutally cut out some more. Strike those "fors," "thes," "becauses," and "thats." Then, ask a friend you trust with a blue pencil to read your story and cut some more before you hand it in. Usually, somebody else can do a better job editing your work than you can.

Dan Sullivan, copy desk chief of the *Chicago Daily News* for more than 20 years, used to edit Mike Royko's column every day, in addition to his other copydesk duties.

When asked if it made him nervous to edit the work of the great—and gruff—Mike Royko, Sullivan always answered, "Even Mike deserves a good editor." It's no insult to have your work corrected, tightened, and checked. It's absolutely vital to accurate, clean copy.

And speaking of master copy editor Dan Sullivan brings up another point. Before you even begin to let your creative juices flow, you must have two books at your elbow that he was never without: a dictionary and a style book.

Following are four releases to be edited and rewritten.

The first excellent release, about the new season-ticket plan at the Candlelight Dinner Playhouse, may be edited entirely with copyediting marks and doesn't require any rewriting.

The next three must be rewritten entirely. Put the important facts in a "lead" paragraph, with the rest of the information following.

EXERCISE 7-1

Edit this:

> Candlelight Dinner Playhouse
>
> CANDLELIGHT DINNER PLAYHOUSE, the popular home of award-winning Broadway Musicals and Fine Dining, is now offering a new Season Ticket Plan which features preferred seating and generous discounts. Best Seats are guaranteed with an $8.00 Discount on each Season Ticket Series.
>
> Other advantages include booking four consecutive shows in advance with prices guaranteed (a true inflation fighter), a choice of six weekly performances, and easy ticket exchanges. The Plan is flexible, even allowing patrons to select four different evenings for their four shows.
>
> CANDLELIGHT will also guarantee and reserve Season Tickets over the phone.
>
> For further information, call CANDLELIGHT'S Box Office, at 458-7373 or visit or write CANDLELIGHT DINNER PLAYHOUSE, 5620 Harlem Avenue, Summit, Illinois, 60501.
>
> -0-

(See the next page for the edited version, but not until you've done your own.)

Candlelight Dinner Playhouse

CANDLELIGHT DINNER PLAYHOUSE, ~~the popular home of award-win-ning Broadway Musicals and Fine Dining,~~ in Summit is ~~now~~ offering a new Season Ticket Plan which features preferred seating and generous discounts. Best Seats are guaranteed with an $8.~~00~~ Discount on each Season Ticket Series.

Other advantages include booking four consecutive shows in advance with prices guaranteed, ~~(a true inflation fighter)~~ a choice of six weekly performances, and easy ticket exchanges. The Plan is flexible, ~~even allowing~~ patrons may select four different evenings ~~for their four shows.~~

CANDLELIGHT will ~~also~~ guarantee and reserve Season Tickets over the phone.

For further information, call CANDLELIGHT'S Box Office, at 458-7373, ~~or visit~~ or write CANDLELIGHT DINNER PLAYHOUSE, 5620 Harlem Avenue, Summit, ~~Illinois~~ IL 60501.

EXERCISE 7-2

Rewrite in one paragraph.

    Nancy's Restaurant

       There will be a Press Party to commemorate the completion of the $50,000 renovation of Nancy's Restaurant in Oak Lawn on Wednesday, November 18, beginning at 6:30 P.M.

       Nancy's Restaurant is located at 4700 W. 103rd Street in Oak Lawn (Arena Shopping Center).

       A formal invitation is following.

       Dave Howey and John Gambino, your hosts, hope that you will be able to join them to see the new attractiveness of this popular restaurant.

(See the rewrite on the next page after you finish.)

David Howey and John Gambino, owners of Nancy's Restaurant, 4700 W. 103rd St., Oak Lawn, in Arena Shopping Center, will hold a press party at 6:30 P.M. Wednesday, Nov. 18, to unveil the restaurant's $50,000 renovation. A formal invitation will follow.

EXERCISE 7-3

Rewrite:

Ben-Allen Productions

Ben-Allen Productions is announcing a special FATHER'S DAY DISCOUNT for their hit musical "Sasha! Sing Dinah!" currently at the Happy Medium, 901 N. Rush Street. Dad gets in for ½ price with your regular price ticket for either the 5:00 P.M. matinee or the 8:00 P.M. evening show on Father's Day, Sunday, June 12. Reservations must be made in advance by calling 443-0177 from 11:00 A.M. to 5:00 P.M. daily. (Noon to 4:00 P.M. Sundays.)

"Sasha! Sing Dinah!" is a musical portrait of Dinah Washington now in its fifth month at the Happy Medium in the heart of Chicago's night-club district. Sasha Dalton stars in the show which also features Don Blackwell, Sulanya Conway, Lenny Lynn, Manuel Arrington and the Corky McClerkin Quartet.

"Sasha! Sing Dinah!" is two solid hours of the best acting, singing, dancing, comedy and music you'll ever see. It is, indeed, a full evening of theatre!

FOR FURTHER INFORMATION CONTACT ALLEN AT 443-0177 or 782-9145

(See the revision on the next page.)

Chicago, Illinois, June 1, 1981—A special half price Father's Day discount for the musical "Sasha! Sings Dinah!" at the Happy Medium has been announced by Ben Allen Productions. On Sunday, June 12, fathers will be admitted to the evening performance for $5 when accompanied by a family member. Advance reservations are required for the 8 P.M. performance and can be made by calling 443-0177 between 11 A.M. and 4 P.M. The Happy Medium is located at 901 N. Rush Street.

The three-hour show features Sasha Dalton in the musical portrayal of singer Dinah Washington.

EXERCISE 7-4

Rewrite into half the length:

PRE-KING RICHARD'S FAIRE WORKSHOPS
BEING OFFERED JUNE 27 TO JULY 1

Artists, craftsmen and the general public are invited to attend any of several free pre-King Richard's Faire workshops being offered June 27 to July 1 by the Renaissance Faire. The workshops are designed to involve and stimulate an awareness of the Renaissance period. The 9th Annual King Richard's Faire—A Return to the Renaissance—is a re-creation of a Renaissance marketplace in England during festival time more than 400 years ago.

"The five workshops will be headed by some of the most noted authorities on the Renaissance period," said John T. Mills, entertainment director of King Richard's Faire. "The Customs and Manners Workshop on June 27 will be taught by Frank Harnish, speech and theatre professor at the College of Lake County and an authority on customs of the period," Mills said. This workshop will concentrate on the historical perspective of customs and manners and will cover everything from manners to witchcraft.

Calligraphy will be offered on June 28 by Nancy Fortunato, a professional watercolorist, author and calligrapher. Fortunato will teach practical applications and different styles of calligraphy.

Peter Draves will head the June 29 workshop on Music of the Renaissance. An accomplished musician in period music, Draves will cover historical and theoretical aspects of Renaissance music. Topics to be covered include madrigal ensembles, wandering minstrels and recorder groups, and various musical styles will be demonstrated.

Costuming of the Renaissance will be offered on June 30. Ellen Kozak, professional costume designer from Milwaukee, will conduct this workshop on individual costume development and the stylistic differences between countries.

Dr. Leslie Hinderyckx, chairman of the Theatre Department at Northwestern University, will offer a workshop on Dialects, July 1. This performance-oriented workshop deals with specific dialects of the Renaissance from both a historical and practical perspective.

All workshops begin at 7:30 P.M. at King Richard's Faire in Bristol Township, Wisc. King Richard's Faire begins July 3, 4 and 5 with the Queen's Coronation and His Majesty's Cross-Country Horse Races, and runs for seven consecutive weekends through August 15 and 16.

King Richard's Faire is located just off I-94 on the Illinois/Wisconsin state line. For further details, contact the Faire office at 312/689-2800 or 414/396-4385.

Chapter 8

Following the Commandments

If you are determined to worship the gods of Journalism and Public Relations, you must follow three commandments.

The first is: *Your facts must always be correct.* Check, check, check—before you write, after you write, when you edit your copy, and after you have somebody else edit it. There's no excuse for an "oops" after publication. An apology the next day doesn't correct the damage an error does to your professional reputation as a fact-gatherer and to the newspaper as a carrier of truth. But also remember that errors happen to all of us, no matter how long we do this work. We are constantly "looking over our shoulders," never too confident to recheck facts over and over. You must never take any facts for granted.

A research associate at *Esquire* magazine, whose job it is to check facts and update and edit stories by nationally acclaimed writers, reports that he spots an average of from two to three mistakes on every short typewritten page he works on. And this is the work of so-called "professional" writers—also known as the cream of the crop.

This young editor cites as an example a story he edited that mentioned a Greek amphitheater. Because he suspected the word "amphitheater" was misspelled, he looked it up in the encyclopedia.

There he learned that in addition to spelling the word incorrectly, the author had misused it. There were no amphitheaters in Greece. People think there were because the Greeks were so involved in the theater. Actually the amphitheaters were in Rome.

I recently received a news release in the mail from a generally reputable publicist. Announcing the opening of a new gourmet food shop, the writer rhapsodized about the new trend toward preparing exotic food for evening carry-out service. The writer also mentioned the trend had grown from the *charcuteries* in France, and cited the most famous *charcuterie* of all: Fanchon. Unfortunately, that place in Paris is spelled *Fauchon*. And if I hadn't checked on the spelling with a native Parisian I know, I would have been pretty embarrassed on publication of the story I wrote based on that release.

The moral of these stories is: Never trust anyone to give you the facts correctly. Double check everything yourself. As Ed Eulenberg, editor at Chicago's City Press and *Daily News,* always warned his newest staff members: "If your mother says she loves you—check on it!"

You have to be careful because somebody—a reader or an editor—will discover your mistakes. In fact, good editors tend to be skeptical about everything they get in the mail by way of press releases—and play detective.

For example, the summer before Prince Charles wedded Lady Diana, most news offices were awash with press releases pertaining to the big event. The British Consul General was particularly excited and was busy alerting everyone in the press to any number of possible news stories.

One release that came over my desk told me that Americans were very interested in the big wedding and that U.S. importers and retail outlets were deluged with requests for wedding paraphernalia. The release claimed Americans were very anxious to buy the memorabilia and enclosed a list of 100 companies that would be possible sources for the royal engagement and wedding commemorative items.

With great interest, I read a story in a Chicago daily newspaper quoting the release almost verbatim.

> By now, everyone in America—and everywhere else—knows that Prince Charles, future king of England, will wed Lady Diana Spencer on July 29 at St. Paul's Cathedral.
>
> But the question was, until recently, does anyone in America care?
>
> The answer is a resounding "You bet," according to U.S. importers and retail outlets who, deluged with requests for wedding paraphernalia, are rushing to cash in on the multi-million dollar commemorative bonanza.

The article said that assumption was based on a quote from the trade promotion spokesman for the British Consul General in Chicago, who said he had had calls from all over the country from people showing an interest in the event.

Next, it quoted Lord Piers Anthony Wedgewood (whose family founded the famous Wedgewood China Company), who was in America for a timely promotion tour of his wedding products.

It ended with the address and phone number of the local consulate, just in case anyone wanted to order something.

The fact of the matter is that at that point in time there was considerably less interest in the event than either the British or the shopkeepers here had anticipated.

When I received that same news release and list, instead of accepting the consulate spokesman's statement as fact, I telephoned every listed retailer and outlet that had a Chicago address. I soon discovered that one of those sources had been out of business for two years. The other four were not planning to order any commemorative items because all felt there "is no particular interest in America in the British memorabilia."

Next, I telephoned the buyers in five Chicago department stores and learned they hadn't noticed any particular interest in the event and were not planning to install large supplies of British wedding memorabilia.

(Later, at the time of the wedding, there was a flurry of interest for a few days but nothing to match the suggestions of the consulate spokesman and the newspaper story.)

It was a perfect example of how you can't trust anything to be accurate until you have checked the facts yourself.

It also shows that you, as a public relations counselor, must be sure that the stories you send out about your clients are accurate. Most reporters and editors are going to check on the facts before printing them in their publications. And if you are wrong, you may do more harm than good to your clients'—and to your own—reputations.

In this instance, the British Consul would have been better off finding people who were really interested in the British throne and focusing on those groups for publicity during the festivities.

The same newspaper carried a story in June 1981 with a clever lead: "School is out for the summer, but while the schools are closing, learning is still in season."

The story introduced the reader to a list of

places where students might go to continue their educations informally during summer. But the writer got so caught up in her fanciful style and depended so uncritically on the news releases that she slipped up on the facts.

First, quoting a release, she announced, the "Chicago Public Library has come up with a new program for students this year which will encourage children to make reading a habit by playing a game."

According to her description of this "new" game, children would be invited to read any book of their choice and then write about it or talk to a library staff member about it. The title of each book read was to be recorded in a log that would indicate the child's progress. For each book read, the story said, the child would spin a number wheel and advance that number of squares on a big board.

Although the writer, quoting her PR release, claimed the game was new, it sounded very familiar to readers who had been reared in Chicago and had played the game, with slight variations, all the summers of their youth.

I called the library's public relations department, asked the writers there to check the facts, and discovered that the summer reading program was more than 50 years old. But that wasn't the only problem in this story.

The writer was so swamped with press releases and so heady with her powers that she had gone on in the same article to make yet another untrue statement. First, she proclaimed that students could also take classes in private schools during the summer if they paid from $200 to $800 for each. That information came from some news releases sent out by private schools—and it was true. However, the reporter finished the story with the question, "Why do private schools cost so much more?" The answer? "Their doors are always open."

Actually, the PR people can't be blamed for that charge. She obviously made it up herself.

A call to the administrators of two such schools showed that—even if the reporter had had any business making such personal observations in a news report—this one was definitely not true.

Keeping doors open has little to do with the high cost of private schools. They cost more because they are not publicly funded; teachers' salaries remain competitive with those in public schools; and the facilities, laboratories, and courses are more expensive than those in public schools because they're geared to the above-average child in smaller classrooms. Also, specialized equipment, such as television sets and complete computer systems, increase operating costs.

The second newswriting commandment is:

Your news must be timely. That means your information must be current or be pertinent to what is happening now. In this business, we're talking about news—not olds. If you can't come up with new information or a new angle on old information, save it for a history book, annual report, or biography.

Keep in mind that timeliness means you must be aware of what's happening in the news, so you can determine what is current and relevant.

For example, a news release about a new book on how to save money on taxes should be on the editors' desks long before April if it's going to get to the consumer before the IRS deadline.

The third commandment is:

You must never miss your deadline. Whether you're a publicist or staff reporter, your story will do no good at all if it comes in after the deadline. There will be a blank space on the page where your news should have been. For example, your client's restaurant will open without your announcement.

It's your personal responsibility to put your bottom in a chair, face the terrible typewriter, and get the story out and onto the editor's desk before the second hand hits deadline. There are no excuses for missing that moment. In fact, many editors and business executives consider it justifiable cause for firing both PR people and reporters.

Part III

The Profile

Chapter 9

Finding a Subject

Rich, famous, and/or powerful people always make interesting profiles. Reporters are eager to write them, and editors are usually eager to print them. Everyone knows that such stories, with photos of well-known subjects, attract readers and sell publications. Perfect examples are found in *People* magazine each week.

But most publications are also interested in profiles of outstanding persons who are at the top of their fields, even though they are more or less unknown to the general public. The heads of Fortune 500 companies, professionals such as doctors and lawyers, and people who have made outstanding contributions can also be exciting to read about.

Sometimes journalists profile a person who has a surprising contrast in his or her life. He may be the head of a multinational corporation who has won acclaim among wildlife enthusiasts for his birdwatching expeditions. The contrast between his two worlds provides an interesting tension in the story.

You may also profile such subjects as cities, foundations, institutions, and corporations.

A profile can be defined as an in-depth view of a person, place, or thing, showing all its sides, so the reader comes away from the story feeling he has a personal, intimate, and complete view of the subject.

As in all stories for news publications, profiles should be timely. There should be some reason for writing a profile of someone or something now.

The 100th birthday of an institution, such as the Institute of Psychoanalysis, is sufficient reason to write such an in-depth study. Winning an important award may make someone newsworthy enough to interview. Unfortunately, death is often the reason for a probing and effective profile.

One of the best examples of the obituary profile was written by Donald Zochert, an author who was formerly an associate editor and reporter for the *Chicago Daily News*, in tribute to nationally renowned Chicago Police Chief O. W. Wilson (see Exhibit 9-1).

After this profile appeared, some members of the journalism staff at Northwestern University asked "Zoch" to write an analysis of how he created the story so they could pass it on to their feature-writing students. Here's his explanation:

1. Give it a hint of Biblical phrasing—not too strong—but enough to suggest something of the context in which Wilson moved and the aura surrounding him.

2. A quote entirely out of context, selected to demonstrate—not overtly state—something of his character.

3. Same purpose here—"He was a Lutheran

EXHIBIT 9-1. Profile: An Obituary.

7 years with 'the Professor'

By Donald Zochert

When O. W. Wilson took over the Chicago Police Department, he did something unusual.

He called a mass meeting of all the city's policemen.

(1) And when they had assembled together, he forgave them their trespasses.

And he warned them not to trespass again.

That was O. W. Wilson.

He came riding out of the West on a rocking horse of righteousness to set Chicago straight.

Goodness knows, Chicago needed setting straight. You couldn't tell the cops from the robbers, people said.

Thus: the Professor.

Austere, flint-eyed, precise to a fault, O. W. Wilson was picked to be the Moses of the Blue Machine, the man to lead Chicago's Police Department out of the wilderness.

(2) "I cannot tolerate such things as doors left ajar," he said. "I have insisted on this throughout the police department."

(3) He was a Lutheran and he didn't go to movies.

O. W. WILSON TOOK OVER the police department in 1960.

(4) He quit in 1967, retiring to California with his wife, his daughter, and a photograph of Richard J. Daley.

(5) The photograph went up on the wall of the den in his home at Poway, Calif., where O. W. Wilson died Wednesday morning, after a massive stroke.

He was 72, composed, he said, to tranquility.

If he left his mark on Chicago—and no one doubts that he did—Chicago left its mark on him.

(6) To a reporter, he quoted Samuel Johnson:

"Praise is to an old man an empty sound. There is little to be feared from the malevolence of men, and yet less to be hoped from their affection or esteem.

"Riches would now be useless, and high employment would be pain."

And then he winked.

SOME SAY IT WAS Richard Daley who brought O. W. Wilson to Chicago, but it was really Richard Morrison, the "babbling burglar."

Morrison's tale of how cops were in cahoots with robbers in the old Summerdale District stoked the fires of scandal in the Police Department, greased the skids for Comr. Timothy J. O'Connor and sent Daley in search of a new police chief.

He named O. W. Wilson chairman of a five-man
(7) committee to conduct the search.

The committee searched and searched. It interviewed scores of persons.

And then it picked one.

O. W. Wilson.

WHATEVER THE MECHANICS of his ascension, O. W. Wilson had the credentials.

He'd been a policeman in Berkeley, Calif., and police chief of Fullerton, Calif.

(8) He'd cleaned up Wichita and he'd taught at Harvard.

He'd been professor of police administration at the University of California, and dean of the school of criminology there.

He'd written books on police work, and one—on police administration—had been translated into Spanish, Arabic, and Chinese.

(9) Like any man who wants the door closed or open but not ajar, administration and organization were his strength.

He'd directed reorganization surveys for police departments in Dallas and San Antonio, Tex., Pasadena, Calif., and Hartford, Conn., in Birmingham, Ala., and Nashville, Tenn., and Louisville, Ky., and Oakland, Calif.

(10) He had a chestful when he came to Chicago, every qualification save one: he hadn't come up through the ranks.

The men in the ranks noticed that.

They didn't like it.

And that was curious.

Because some of the men in the ranks—the newspaper called them "honest policemen"—complained that a man couldn't rise in the ranks unless he knew someone, or paid someone. If you made it you were crooked, they said.

But O. W. Wilson paid no mind.

Ten days after he took office as superintendent, he called his men together, granted absolution for sins past, and laid down the law

(11) Then he straightened his tie and went to work.

He ordered a reduction in police districts, from the 38 in existence when he took over, to only 21.

Efficiency, he said.

Dynamite, said his opponents.

EXHIBIT 9-1 (Continued)

The people in the neighborhoods, said his opponents, want a police station within walking distance of their homes.

They'll have a police officer within seconds of their homes, he said.

What no one said is that O. W. Wilson had broken up the little kingdoms of district captains, had cut one link between policemen and the apples of temptation.

EVEN MORE CONTROVERSIAL, he established a special watchdog group known as the Internal Investigations Division, policemen for policemen.

He hired women to direct traffic at school crossings.

⑫ He doubled the number of civilians in clerical jobs.

He freed regular police officers for duty on patrol.

Faced with an antiquated communications system—sometimes it took an hour for an officer to respond to a call for assistance—he tackled the problem of efficiency on the street.

He installed a sophisticated and expensive ($2 million) communication network.

To make it work, he nearly doubled the number of squad cars.

And to make that work, he installed the one-man squad car.

Even today, officers get their hackles up over one-man squad cars.

Unsafe, they say.

Not so, Wilson said. With instant radio communications, no officer would be more than a few seconds from help. But he conceded: there are some neighborhoods where two-man squad cars are "absolutely necessary."

His seven year shakeup took other turns:

- He applied computer technology to police statistics, crime records and departmental planning.
- He added a canine force.
- He modernized the crime laboratory.
- He sent supervisors back to school for more training.
- He standardized the police uniform.
- He won salary increases for his men.
- And for the first time since 1948, he reopened the promotion examinations system.

MORE: HE RUBBED THE tarnish off Chicago's police star. By the time he finished, Chicago enjoyed the reputation of having one of the nation's most efficient, highly trained and professional police departments.

⑬ Through it all, O. W. Wilson remained himself: austere, unruffled, particular.

To his close associates on the force, he was O.W., a man of strict temperament and sly humor.

⑭ To his wife, he was "Win," for the Winston in Orlando Winston Wilson.

To many of the men on the force, he was still an outsider.

Even in death, there was dissent.

"Few men have contributed so much to the people of Chicago as he did," Mayor Daley said in his condolence to Wilson's family.

"He was an able administrator," said Joseph
⑮ Pecoraro, president of the Chicago Patrolman's Assn., in an interview. But then Pecoraro added,

"The one-man squad cars were bad. He took the detectives out of the district stations, and that was bad. He consolidated the districts.

"All of these things moved the police further from the people. It drove us completely away from the people."

BUT FOR O. W. Wilson, these differences were things left behind. They were the "pain of high employment."

He was 60 years old when he came to Chicago, 67 when he left. This was his swan song.

At rest in California, with his wife at his side, he turned to growing flowers.

⑯ And when Bob Rose, West Coast bureau chief for The Daily News, visited him there, O. W. Wilson insisted on reading from Samuel Johnson.

"I think Johnson was talking about me," he said.

And then he read:

"I leave many great designs unattempted and many great attempts unfinished. My mind is burdened with no heavy crime, and therefore, I compose myself to tranquility . . . expect, with serene humility, that hour which nature cannot long delay, and hope to possess in a better state that happiness which here I could not find and that virtue which here I have not attained."

He was, after all, The Professor.

and he didn't go to movies." These things have nothing to do with each other; putting them together in one short sentence like this arrests the attention. It emphasizes them as evidence of character.

4. Once again, a device to arrest the attention—starting out with what a man is expected to retire with—a wife, a child—and ending with the unexpected.

5. Then that unexpected photograph is used to bring in the fact of Wilson's death.

6. They dropped a paragraph here introducing the quote—added in later editions: "To a reporter, he quoted Samuel Johnson:"

7. You would probably call this an inverted pyramid or an amorphous rectangle. I don't call it anything, except I present a general idea and go to a specific fact, reducing the length of the sentences to sort of zero in on the fact: They picked Wilson.

8. "He cleaned up Wichita" instead of "He became chief of police in Wichita, Kan., and within five years was credited with cleaning up the city's scandal-ridden police force. He was eventually fired, and claimed his dismissal was the result of politics." The purpose: simplify, simplify. "He cleaned up Wichita" has a ring of the righteous sheriff of the Old West.

9. Here I pull in a thread started in Note 2 above, hopefully giving a little cohesion to a long tale.

10. He had a chestful of what? Well—a chestful of medals, let's say, of meritorious service. But by not spelling it out, there is also the suggestion of a chest puffed with pride and self-righteousness.

11. He straightened his tie instead of rolling up his sleeves. I'm not above the cliche—that should be obvious (I think they're good sometimes, when they're intentional)—but this is the opposite side of a cliche. And a clue, once again, to the strict and prim streak in his character.

12. Run what he did without comment (although I slipped and commented on the consolidation of police districts). The purpose here is not to judge what he did, but to simply state what he did. Not to eulogize his actions, but to describe them. The reader can then decide for himself whether Wilson did anything worthwhile. To me, the list is impressive, if only by its length.

13. Back here to O.W. the man, the basis of the story.

14. Work in his full name—people wonder about that—without being blatant.

15. Demonstrate—if possible without taking sides—that Wilson had his opposition (for whatever motives) and that there was a difference of opinion on whether some of his changes were good or bad. It would certainly be telling the truth but only part of the truth if this sort of thing was not alluded to.

16. Having quoted from Rose's interview with Wilson earlier, and now about to quote from it again, at least give Rose credit as unobtrusively as possible—i.e., here rather than earlier in the story.

There were two chief purposes behind the writing. To recount what Wilson had done as police superintendent was necessary, but I also wanted to get into the story some suggestion of the man himself. In other words, I think people can read this and say not only that O. W. Wilson was police superintendent (an image, a function) but that O. W. Wilson was a specific man with a certain character—just as the reader himself is a specific person.

The other purpose was not to eulogize Wilson. No police superintendent ever had a better press. His image was that of a man of virtue. Clean. Yet he also went on free junkets, got involved in politics, and snooped on the coppers who opposed him. To go back a bit, before Note 2, where I call him the "Moses of the Blue Machine, the man to lead Chicago's Police Department out of the wilderness." Some readers will take that as a straight (and correct) judgment of the man; but by propping it up with the 'Blue Machine' and the double allusion to Moses I would hope that other readers might ask: Is the writer really serious?

In other words, I wanted a straight—although still readable—story.

In August 1982, when the stock market and interest rates were in a turmoil, Robert A. Bennett of the *New York Times* wrote a remarkable profile of Henry Kaufman, whose predictions influence the economy.

Although Bennett didn't speak with Kaufman (who declined requests for an interview), he managed to get all the information he needed from fans and foes.

His story began brightly with a catchy lead: "When Henry Kaufman talks, the financial markets move. That, at least, is how it has been." Then it continued:

Take Tuesday. With a dramatic reversal of his earlier predictions, that interest rates would rise to new peaks, Mr. Kaufman sparked tumult in the stock and bond markets. Bond prices soared and the Dow Jones industrial average jumped a record 38.81 points in one of the heaviest trading days in history.

But some economists are predicting that the latest Kaufman rally may be his last, and that the image of the Salomon Brothers chief economist may have faded as the result of his newly found relative optimism.

EXERCISE 9-1

Write a brief analysis of Donald Zochert's story on O. W. Wilson. Discuss the lead. Does it work? Why? How are quotes used? How do they enhance the spinning of this remarkable yarn? Where are the facts? Is there anything special or unusual about the writer's skill in weaving them in and around the fanciful descriptions?

Is there another way to tell this story in a one paragraph, five-W news report? Do that below.

Why isn't that treatment good enough for this particular event?

Chapter 10

Doing Your Homework

— *Profile*

Although the profile is, like the press release and the feature story, dependent on good, solid research of all kinds, it is based primarily on one research tool in particular: the interview. In addition, the interview is often the main thread from which an entire news or feature story can be woven. Whether you are writing about a new product, fighting a rumor about the imminent demise of the company, reporting on the economic views of the chairman of the board, or doing a profile of the new plant manager, you must learn how to conduct an interview. After all, it's the only way you can tap your most valuable source of information—people.

It's important to remember that there are very few bad story ideas. There are only writers with too little imagination to make them good. When you sit eyeball to eyeball with your interviewee, your story should begin to come alive. Whether it's about a Gillette razor or a Holiday Inn hotel room, a true professional should be able to get an idea and make it work—with the help of a good interview. In order to perform that trick, however, you must have a positive attitude and the confidence that you can do the job. You also need some insight into *how* you can do it. The key is to muster up lots of energy and enthusiasm. That will keep you digging until you've turned up some interesting facts. You will also need a sharp eye that helps you find colorful details to spark up an otherwise bland tale.

A perfect example is the *New York Times* story by Michael Norman about how the New York State Lotto game is luring more players. The story idea isn't exactly a barn burner, but Norman pitched in with enthusiastic interviews, then wrote a fetching report that began with an anecdote about a Lotto player:

> Just after noon yesterday, Fred Christ, a high school teacher from Union, N.J., and at first glance a seemingly straightforward, plain-speaking and sensible man, stepped up to the Lotto booth on the second floor of the Port Authority Bus Terminal to buy his weekly ticket.
>
> Like millions of other people who play the game, he knew his fate turned on chance, on ping-pong balls dropping randomly from a rotating drum. . . .
>
> "I was reading in the Book of Revelations in the Bible the other day and I

played the first six numbers I read," he said. "You can't get a higher authority than that."

A classic example of how a reporter turned what might have been a boring story into a lively feature full of interesting facts is the following article, which appeared in the late *Chicago Daily News*—and did a very positive public relations job for the Ritz-Carlton Hotels.

Written by Henry Hanson, it was about the opening of Chicago's Ritz-Carlton. The doors had not yet officially opened, and there was nobody there to talk to except the manager. Yet, the public relations person invited Henry to interview the chairs, the chandeliers, the elevators, and even the wine cellar for this delightful piece (see Exhibit 10-1).

Henry breathes life into a near-empty building with his skillful blending of fanciful observations, whimsical musings, and hard, clear, accurate facts.

Note that his short, simple lead sums up the ambience of all the Ritz-Carlton hotels and lets his readers know what's coming.

He slips some news in—about the splendid wine cellar and other special features that were new to the city at that time—to remind his readers it's a news story, not an essay.

To bring in people where there are none, Henry dredges up long-dead Charles Ritz and quotes him. He also drops in some pithy comments by the hotel manager and lets us smile at some of his anecdotes.

When you've finished the article, you've learned more than you probably wanted to know about the Ritz chain—but you've had great fun doing it.

Before going for the actual interview you must do your homework. As mentioned in Chapter 1, you must contact everyone you know—and even some people you don't know—who have or might have some information about your subject.

Once you have decided whom to interview, get your hands on any newspaper or magazine articles by or about them. Visit the library and newspaper files to track these down. Most libraries will give you hard copies of newspaper

stories for a small fee. Get a copy of the company's annual report. Find as many tangible facts as possible. That will keep you from digging for facts that are already public knowledge. And if you exhibit such knowledge at the interview, it will help win respect from your interviewee.

How embarrassing it would be to ask, "And how is your wife?" only to hear, "We were divorced last week. It was in all the newspapers." Worse would be to ask the interviewee how many children he has—only to learn he was moved to found a sterility clinic because of his infertility.

Simple research should follow these outlines:

- If you are writing about a company, check with people who do business with it, such as suppliers, banks, and customers.

- If your subject is an individual, check the Who's Who books as well as personal and business associates.

- Call people who live near the person or place, and ask these neighbors if they've noticed anything of interest about your subject.

- Check with the *Readers Guide to Periodical Literature* in the library to find any recent magazine articles that have been printed about your subject.

By the time you've called several people, read all the background material, and become somewhat familiar with your subject, you should begin to feel the excitement and enthusiasm I described earlier. And that will help turn your story from a lemon into "lemonade."

By now, you should also be thinking about some angle you can feature. For after learning about your subject, you'll begin to form some opinions about it. That helps you determine which aspects to highlight. Sometimes, it will make you want to change or minimize some points.

That was the case, you recall, in the Dial soap polluting problem.

All this preparation should also cause a tingling to start in your bloodstream and probably

EXHIBIT 10-1. Profile: A Place.

A Ritz to call Chicago's own

By Henry Hanson

The key words at the Ritz-Carlton—soon to be Chicago's newest luxury hotel—are "understated elegance."

Two years of tasting have gone into its 25,000-bottle wine cellar. Select guests will receive gift bottles of chilled champagne. There's a bidet in every corner suite. The china is thin. The press center has a makeup lounge for presidential candidates.

The elevator operators—remember elevator operators?—will wear tight white gloves. Waiters in pantries on each floor will know how to boil a three minute egg (boiled eggs don't travel well if they must be sent up from the kitchen).

There's a kennel for your dog, a chauffeur's lounge so you can find your chauffeur, and a new view of the top of John Hancock Center through the skylight—as you float on a rubber raft nursing a Dubonnet-on-the-rocks in the pool just off the 11th floor sauna.

As Charles Ritz used to say, "The guest is always right—even if we have to throw him out."

IT HAS BEEN A LONG TIME (Lisbon, 1927) since the world has seen a new Ritz Hotel rise, so the owners want to let the pedigree show.

As Cornelius Hackl and Barnaby Tucker sang when they nipped off to New York in "Hello Dolly":

"Middle class . . . don't speak of it,
Savoire-faire . . . we reek of it.
Some were born with rags and patches, but
We use dollar bills for matches and . . .
We've got elegance.
We were born with elegance."

Check-in date at the elegant new Ritz-Carlton is Dec. 1, but there will be no grand opening extravaganza. Guests will just waft down the rose-colored carpeted halls of this well-bred Shangri-la as if it had been waiting for them all along.

"A jet-set opening is not our style," explained William Ebersol, senior vice president and general manager. "The first new Ritz-Carlton in so many years is itself the event.

"Oh, I suppose if Mayor Daley really WANTED to snip a ribbon, we could arrange an occasion. But it's not our style to put on big things."

EBERSOL, A BOYISH 52, explained "the Ritz mystique" in an interview in his 24th-floor Hancock Center office. He wore Gucci loafers, a subdued Countess Mara tie and was seated by a telephone with his name engraved on a gold-plated receiver as he worried about a headline saying: "Chicago Ritz To Open Soon With Due Snobbery."

"The snobbery part made headlines, but we're not snobbish," he declared. "If some of our guests are regarded as snobs, OK. I'm not going to quarrel with that."

The Ritz mystique is a combination of flawless service and fastidious design, befitting the wealthy clientele it hopes to attract to the hotel on floors 11 through 31 of the 74-story Water Tower Place.

Ebersol comes down the Beacon Hill pike to Chicago after nine years at the helm of Boston's snooty Ritz-Carlton Hotel where . . .

EXHIBIT 10-1 (Continued)

- "We had to tell one of President Kennedy's brothers to keep his feet off the table in the bar. And that reporter with him, too!"
- "All of Boston's protest parades marched right in front of the hotel, but they didn't give us any trouble, and we didn't give them any trouble."
- "Julia Child eats there on a regular basis. Churchill stayed there. So does Prince Rainier and Beverly Sills and Ann Landers, who always wants fresh fruit in her room."

BOSTON'S RITZ-CARLTON is the only other hotel to bear the name in the United States. Others—all named simply The Ritz, except for Montreal's Ritz-Carlton—are in Madrid, London, Barcelona, Lisbon and Paris, where it all began. . . .

Neighbors up and down the street are first-rate—Saks, Tiffany's, Gucci's, and the new Lord & Taylor and Marshall Field & Co. stores. Neiman-Marcus hopes to move in soon.

EBERSOL SAID HE BECAME truly impressed with the Magnificent Mile not long ago: "It was midnight. I was walking along Michigan Av. There on the corner were two bank presidents, the president of an insurance company and the president of a big real estate firm—standing there discussing business at midnight! Can you imagine this happening anywhere else?

"The city works," he added, easing into the cliche of the day.

A few other Ritz-Carlton notes:

- All 600 employes will move in for a night on the house to better understand the Ritz mystique.
- A ratio of at least three employes for every two guests will be maintained. "It will be a 5-, 6-, or 7-to-1 ratio when we're less than full," said Ebersol.
- Walls will be twice as thick as in other hotels.
- Push buttons will summon waiters in all guest rooms.
- Credit cards will be accepted—a grudging departure from the Boston Ritz-Carlton's ban on credit cards.
- The Greenhouse will feature tropical foliage, babbling waterfalls, soft moss—and gin, if you wish.

IN ANY MULTIMILLION-DOLLAR endeavor there are, of course, disappointments.

One is the giant tapestry that had been planned for the Ritz-Carlton lobby—a replica of a large part of the Art Institute's Georges Seurat masterpiece "Sunday Afternoon on the Island of La Grande Jatte."

Ebersol explained, "Leigh Block (Art Institute board chairman) had OKd the plan. We wanted to have the tapestry done in France. But negotiations dragged on and on for so long . . . We were finally talked out of it."

Then Ebersol pulled from his coat pocket a postcard reproduction of "La Grande Jatte" and ruefully mused, "I still hope that maybe someday . . ."

Meanwhile, smile, Chicago, and shove aside the potted palms because the band is about to strike up Irving Berlin's "Puttin' on the Ritz"—Chicago style.

create some nervousness too. This feeling is akin to an actor's stage fright. It's quite natural to fear you're not fully prepared, that you may not get all the necessary answers in your first interview, and—Horrors!—you may have to call back and fill in with some more questions the following day.

Probably the most important thing to do here is to stop and reassure yourself that even the most seasoned professional has "interview fright" before the big game. No matter how long we do it, and no matter how carefully we prepare for the interview, there's always a feeling, deep down, that this may be the one that isn't going to work.

What you have to do is acknowledge that self-doubt. Then, reassure yourself that with proper preparation your chance of success is probably insured. Be grateful you're not the photographer who never has that second chance to shoot after the home run's been hit. We can always stop back and ask the player how it felt.

It's my personal feeling, after more than 20 years of interviewing, that this little touch of "interview fright" before the actual meeting makes me perform better. It keeps me from being too sure of myself. It keeps me trying harder.

After you have properly backgrounded yourself, sit down and write a list of ten questions. These will help to prevent that uncomfortable pause when you can't think of anything to ask your client in the interview.

There's a good chance you'll never have to look at this list of questions. It's possible your subject will be so verbose he or she will just chatter away, hitting on all the important points in order, as you scribble down the answers. But, in truth, I've rarely seen that happen.

Sometimes, just one or two simple questions warm both of you up and start the conversation. Soon you're chatting so excitedly and intelligently you *do* cover every issue. And at the end of such a successful meeting, you look back over your questions and find that you have the answers to all of them.

That will happen often when the interviewee is a very congenial person, you are very well informed, and you make friends with each other upon meeting.

Know at the start that there are some clients who are not going to cooperate with you. Sometimes you are going to strike out.

I will never forget my own worst interview.

It happened when I met with an elderly, world-famous psychiatrist who had just had a new book published. He was touring the country on a publicity tour, and his public relations counselor telephoned my newspaper requesting the interview.

I went to the newspaper library and read all the stories written about him. Next, I read his new book—although, admittedly, I had some trouble understanding many of the erudite sections in it.

I had such great respect for this old gentleman—and was in such awe of him—that I was very careful to prepare what I considered informed, intelligent questions that would let him know I'd done my homework.

Unfortunately, when we finally met, he had just come from a television interview with Barbara Walters, and her direct approach had definitely upset him. Twice he mentioned that interview to me, adding, "I bet you're one of those tough lady reporters like Barbara Walters."

Henry Herr Gill, nationally acclaimed *Chicago Daily News* photographer who later became head of the *Sun-Times'* photo department, had come with me and was more relaxed than I, so he accepted the drink our host offered. I didn't because I was too busy getting my questions ready and setting out my papers and pencils. We had just started serious business, when the gentleman again offered me a drink—and again I refused.

It was just about that time when I realized that I had a very grumpy interviewee sitting across the table—and that he was not being very gracious about answering me.

When I asked what he meant by a certain phrase in his book, he snapped, "What's the matter? Can't you read?" Another time, when I asked a question about his philosophy of life, he said shortly, "That's in the book. Why don't you read it?"

I tried another tack. Drawing from the clippings I'd read about his personal life and his early days as a struggling physician, I asked questions about his family and his colleagues. He cut me off at the pass with "That's all been written before. Why don't you go read that in the library?"

At my wit's end, I said "goodbye" and left the apartment close to tears. Henry laughed when we got outside and said, "You dummy! Why the hell didn't you take the old guy's drink? If you had taken one, he could have. He was so nervous about being interviewed he really needed one, but he was probably afraid that if he took it you'd think he was a lush."

That had never occurred to me, but since that day I've never refused anything my interviewees offer. I don't always eat the homemade cookies, I rarely sip the herbal tea, and I never drink the Scotch while working. But I take them all and let them sit at my elbow, so my subject is free to relax.

Chapter 11

Conducting the Interview

Usually, your interviewee will try to cooperate, and you'll both come away winners.

The biggest key to successful interviewing is to put people at ease. Even if you are their paid publicist, working on their side, the idea of revealing personal feelings may be discomfiting to them.

Try to remember that no matter how important people are, they're still usually unnerved by the unknown, and many of them have never been interviewed before.

Start with the attitude that you'll make peace with instant magic, immediate love. Know that you're going to have to become intimate immediately. Those of us who can do that try to make our subjects feel safe and secure the moment we make our first eye contact. And if you are able to do that, you'll have more success at interviewing than a prima donna interviewer who is more concerned with his or her own comfort.

In this work, it helps to have what is defined as an objective personality—one that's good with other people—rather than a subjective personality—one that prefers to work alone. While investigative reporters and rewrite men can work excellently with subjective personalities, those of us who make a living interviewing have to be able to walk into the room with a smile and a sincere handshake and show a real concern for and interest in people.

We have a better chance of creating a friendly, trusting atmosphere immediately. And that's important because most of us have only a short time for our interviews. There's rarely a "warm-up" period, so we must make instant friendship with a stranger. It must also be strong enough to allow us to ask blunt questions when necessary.

There are some exceptions, of course. I was amused to read the following quote in a personality profile of Richard Dreyfuss by Gene Siskel, movie critic of the *Chicago Tribune*.

"All that an interviewer has to do with Richard Dreyfuss is wait," wrote Mr. Siskel. "Eventually the 34-year-old actor will strip away his standard answers to standard questions, explode in a creative rage and tell you fascinating things about himself as well as the movie business."

He goes on to explain that Dreyfuss was in Chicago to promote his latest film and that city was his sixth stop on a slam-bang, two-week tour in a private jet. Siskel continued:

85

Dreyfuss and I had three separate conversations here on three different days, and his answers continued to get better and better. For example, during the third day of our conversation he revealed the following:

- That he loves the movie, "Whose Life Is It Anyway?" but that he hates his performance.

- That he hasn't had a commercial hit since "The Goodbye Girl," and needs one to keep himself working, rather than for the money "because all they care about in Hollywood is how have your films done lately."

- That a good chunk of the credit for his own movie stardom can be attributed to two surprising sources, "luck" and "not getting married."

I don't know many reporters or public relations people who enjoy the luxury of spending three days sitting around chatting with the persons they are interviewing. Usually, the subjects are too busy to let you hang around and "wait until he tells you fascinating things about himself and his business."

Moreover, most of us wouldn't spend that much time gathering the lackluster information Mr. Siskel used in his lead.

After one day of that conversation, I'd have picked up my notebook, gone back to the office, and started contacting some other people who know and work with the star, in order to make the story more than a one-dimensional report.

So, how do those of us who have to interview "against the clock" create immediate friendship?

Think in terms of sharing and trading stories, when you begin.

Start with a friendly smile; then begin to swap stories with your "new pal." You tell him something about your own life, and wait until he begins to identify with that. Soon his eyes will light up and he'll say, "Of course, something like that happened to me once."

You *must* gain his confidence, for I believe that is indispensable to every successful interview. The subject must like and trust you, in order to let you crawl into his head and steal his thoughts—and often his feelings.

For example, I remember interviewing singer Tom Jones one night immediately after one of his performances. He was backstage with his manager, groupies, assistants, and musicians. They were clustered around the bar, and it looked as though his life was very glamorous and exciting.

We chatted a while, and I traded some stories, telling him about some of my own vulnerabilities, fears, and insecurities. Then I asked if there was anything that frightened him. By then, he felt very safe with me, and in that charming Welsh voice he murmured, "Yes. I'm afraid that one day I may be old and sick." I asked what made him so fearful of that—since we all grow old. Then I wondered aloud if he'd ever been seriously ill.

"Indeed I was," the deep voice rumbled. "When I was a child, I got the lung fever, and I remember I had to stay home in bed a whole year. Every day I looked out the window and watched the other children running up the mountain in our village to play. . . . I remember that and I don't want to be left behind again—while the others go off to play."

In all the interviews this world-famous entertainer had given, the subject of his fears had never before been mentioned. But because the atmosphere of our interview was conducive to the expression of honest, sincere feelings, he felt safe enough to talk about an important incident in his childhood. I came away with a very full pack of interesting information Tom Jones had provided in answer to my questions. Best of all, I had stories that nobody had ever heard before. And you mustn't forget that, in news or PR, that's our first goal: to gather new information.

Another vitally important part of interviewing is learning to listen. And, when you think about it, that's something most of the world doesn't bother to do.

Too often people are so concerned only with what they're saying that they lose interest in what's being said around them. An interviewer cannot afford to do that.

Professionals listen to every word the interviewee says.

If they are very good, they also note attitudes, tones, expressions, and feelings the subject isn't even aware he is showing. Being perceptive enough to pick up such details will give the reporter an added dimension when he sits down to write the story.

And that brings up the subject of tape recorders.

I know they have been the vogue for several years, but, except for rare occasions, I skip them. If the information is extremely delicate or may involve lawsuits later, I place a tape recorder on the table for everyone's protection and then forget about it. I use my notebook for notes as usual. Later, if I need to defend myself, I have the tape available.

In general, I avoid using tape recorders because:

- It takes a lot of time to transcribe the tapes, and you must go over so much material to find specific quotes.

- They make interviewees nervous. When some people realize they're talking into a tape recorder, they become self-conscious and begin talking in funny, stiff, perfect sentences, which are nothing like their natural conversations. This self-consciousness often interferes with their train of thought.

- When you use a tape recorder, you may begin to read off your questions without bothering to listen carefully to the answers, since they are locked on the tape. That can be a dangerous pitfall for a reporter. We've all seen television interviewers doing that. And it's very embarrassing to see them rattle off a question that the guest answered five minutes before.

- I've seen writers return from a taped interview, sit down to start writing a story, and then slap their foreheads in dismay when they realize the battery wasn't working and there's no interview on the tape. Because they thought the tape had been running, they didn't take any notes and didn't listen carefully to the person they were talking to.

So, I and many other professionals depend primarily on our note-taking skill. We also listen to everything the subject says and develop new questions from the answers. I try to be unobtrusive about my note-taking. I keep the notebook on my lap and use the smallest pad I can find. If the subject sees a giant tablet on the table under his nose, it's liable to make him as nervous as a microphone would.

It should be noted, however, that many journalists sit down and write their stories without much more than a glance at the copious notes they took. They sometimes go back and read the notes over for key words and expressions that will recreate the entire interview in their minds. But then many of them find they can develop almost total recall of the session and can write with great feeling from their "mental overview" of the session.

Chapter 12

Asking the Right Questions

If your firm has just taken on a new client and you're going to do the initial interview for the press kit, you must begin by reading the company's annual report. Be aware of who all the principals in the company are. Find out everything you can about the company's most recent business dealings. Then ask such questions as the following:

- What is the latest, most important development?

- Is there a new acquisition, a new investment, a new partner, a new department, new research, or a new building plan?

- Who is really controlling this company?

- Who started the company? When and how did they do it?

- What was the initial investment? How many partners? How was the power divided?

- What was the company's original marketing strategy?

- How and why has it changed, and how long has that taken?

- What are the current marketing strategies and retailing innovations?

- What problems and challenges has the company come up against, and how has it reacted? Has it had to restructure itself in the face of hard times? What do you view as your most difficult problem—and how are you planning to solve it?

- How big is this company, how many employees has it, and what are the overhead costs?

- Are there any new advertising campaigns planned?

- Have you any new products in the works? When will we see them?

While most business people try to evade hard questions about money—there are ways to get estimates. Your client should be warned that reporters will ask about the annual gross revenues. If the subject won't tell them that, reporters will ask if it's "more than $4 million or less than $4 million," and they can usually get somewhere near the ballpark figure.

Also, both the PR counselor and reporter should find out what audience the company is reaching for and whether that has changed significantly in the last few years. This could indicate some newsworthy changes in the company's policy.

While preparing a client for the interview with the press, look around the building and see if there are any areas that might be used as attractive settings for magazine or newspaper stories—and suggest them.

Sometimes a pretty landscaped garden behind corporate offices can be used as a setting for color fashion, home-furnishing, or food photographs—and your company will get a credit line.

Also, check on whether or not there are any unusual people in the company who might become subjects for feature stories in trade publications, community newspapers, or the daily press or on radio and television stations. For example, if the chief executive is a world-class chef, he might make a very good interviewee for the weekly food pages.

The same holds true if one of the maids in a hotel your company owns is working her way through college—where she was named Miss Campus Queen last season. Don't miss it if the vice president of marketing happens to be a flight instructor at a local airfield or if the president of the company slips over to the children's hospital twice a week after work to read stories to the youngsters there.

All of those items might work into very pleasant and positive feature stories for your client.

After your initial interview, try to think in terms of all the media and write several releases, each highlighting the issue that might interest the individual editor, instead of one blanket, general release. That's what I would do—yet I don't know any public relations counselors who bother to do it.

Recently, I did a story about business people who were becoming part-time landlords because, at that time, buying real estate seemed to be a better investment than buying stocks.

Some of the questions I asked several "part-time landlords" were:

- How does one get into real estate—how did you do it?
- What are the three different kinds of real estate people purchase to rent?
- How do you go about finding worthwhile property?
- What should you look for?
- Can you trust your own judgment, or should you get some experts to go shopping with you?
- How can you find such an expert that you can trust?
- How much is this property going to cost, and how can one small investor finance the project?
- How much can you expect to pop up in unforeseen costs once you own the property?
- Once it's yours, how much can you do yourself to keep it in good shape—and when should you call in professional workmen to do repairs?
- Once the property is "tenant-ready," how do you go about renting it?
- Where do you advertise, and how much does advertising cost?
- How do you pick and choose a tenant, how do you check on him, and is that any guarantee he'll pay the rent?
- What's the best thing that's come out of your real estate investments?
- What are the worst things that have happened to you as a part-time landlord?
- Knowing what you know now, would you do it again and are you planning to? What will you buy next and why?
- What are you going to do differently next time?

When you approach the president of the company for an individual interview for a personality profile, you must have a different approach than you would for a general story about the company.

Here you may have to get some biographical details from the personnel department or *Who's Who*. But they rarely have much information about the "human" side of your subject.

Assume you already have the personnel data: his name (and please spell it correctly), age, home address, schooling, previous employment record, and description of his current job.

Now, find out about his family life, personal views, and business philosophy:

- Wife's name, children, ages, what they are doing.

- Personal interests and special projects. Often a pet charity or organization to which he devotes personal time may lead to a feature story.

- How did he happen to join this company? What did he do elsewhere that caught this company's attention—and does he plan to repeat some of those strategies here?

- How did he happen to get into this line of work? Usually, somewhere, way back, something shaped the development of his personal goals. Was there a role model who influenced him? Who was that, and how was he influenced?

- What is his personal business style and how has he developed it?

- What does he believe to be the most important decision of his life?

- What does he believe was the one lucky break that sent him on his way—and what was the biggest mistake?

- Where does he hope to have taken this company in five years?

- In ten years, where does he hope to be professionally and personally? How is he going to accomplish that?

- Has he made a trade off in his personal life for professional success? Given another chance, would he sacrifice some career goals—and spend more time at home?

EXERCISE 12-1

List two of your company's clients and write ten questions that you would ask principals of each in preparation of the first general news release.

EXERCISE 12-2

Now, list ten questions you would ask the president of each company for a personality profile.

Your questions will differ from the questions in Exercise 12-1 in that they will be more personal and more specific. While the general questions deal with industry problems and how the company plans to solve them, these questions will deal exclusively with the individual.

EXERCISE 12-3

Combine all of the skills you have learned so far by interviewing the person sitting next to you.

This exercise should give you an opportunity to develop an "instant friendship" and practice interviewing, note-taking, and writing.

Begin by asking the following questions (and any others you might like to add to them):

1. What's your name, age, and address? (Check spelling and numbers.)

2. Where do you live?

3. Do you live alone?

4. With whom do you live? (Get names, ages, and relationships.)

5. Where do you come from—city, state, schools?

6. Describe your parents and siblings. How many people in your family? What do they do? What kind of home and neighborhood did you grow up in? What are your personal interests and hobbies? How did they develop?

7. What do you do for a living?

8. Is that what you are trained to do? How did you get into that line of work?

9. Is that what you want to do for the rest of your life?

10. What are your goals? Your dreams?

11. What do you think was the most important decision you ever made? Did you decide wisely?

12. Where do you plan to be in ten years?

13. If you could relive your life, what would you do differently?

14. What was the best thing that ever happened to you—and the worst?

Read the answers over several times and mark sections with colored pencils. Think about the most interesting things you have learned about this person. Organize the facts, putting the most important facts first, and write a story. Try for 500 words.

Chapter 13

Writing a Profile

The best way to explain how to write a profile is to show you—step by step—how I developed one of mine.

This example is a story about Bruce Petsche, president of Peerless Metal Industries, Inc., in Bridgeview, Illinois.

At first glance, Petsche is not unusual enough to be profiled in any publication. He appears to be just one more president of one more small, family-owned company that's been moderately successful for 20 years.

But a closer look reveals that Petsche is a unique person, with several contrasts in his life, as well as strong commitments and unusual interests.

One of the timely features of the story was that it revealed his views of unions and manufacturing plant moves to the sunbelt when those issues were becoming extremely important to the State of Illinois.

The tip to do the story came from a reporter on our staff who met Petsche while she was profiling the governor. She was impressed with Petsche's actions as the representative for small business in the Illinois Manufacturers Association and suggested that I talk with him.

She was struck by the fact that he had a very unusual "other life" too—as actor, musician, and writer—and often used those skills to raise money for such organizations as the League of Women Voters.

In addition, Petsche was a bright and highly quotable man, she said, and heavily involved in family and community affairs. We felt that he added up to a perfect profile candidate for *Crain's Chicago Business*.

I telephoned to make an appointment for an interview and was pleasantly surprised to find Petsche happy to interrupt a sales meeting to talk with me. He was delighted over the idea of a story—because he thought it would be fun— and volunteered to help in any way he could.

I explained I was beginning to do some "homework" on him and asked if he had some biographical information that would help—a list of his accomplishments, newspaper clippings, reviews of plays or music he'd written.

He agreed to mail them to me so that I could study them before our meeting the following week. I also planned to telephone some of his fellow members on the IMA to verify our reporter's first impressions of Petsche.

Imagine my surprise and delight when, two hours later, the door of our office burst open and Bruce Petsche bounced in, humming a tune and carrying a briefcase filled with clippings and papers.

Caught off guard, I took him into our conference room where we had our first informal chat.

We became instant friends and talked for more than an hour about where he'd grown up, where he had gone to college, how old he was,

EXHIBIT 13-1. Profile: Bruce Petsche.

Petsche finds time for work, music and fellow men

By Sandra Pesmen

Forty-nine-year-old Bruce Petsche, president of Peerless Metal Industries Inc. in Bridgeview, spends his days perfecting a machine to process hams. Then he spends his evenings being one.

Most of the time this wiry, energetic wonder—who's brought his company from six employees and sales of $158,000 in 1958 to 120 employees today with revenues of $8 million—can be found in his shop overseeing final touches on a revolutionary new machine that compresses bits of boned ham into boneless formed smoked ham.

But when the day's work is done, Bruce rushes home to get ready for his equally important career in music.

The western suburbanite writes and performs in musical plays and satirical political skits, plays five-string guitar and mandolin with a group called the "Brush Hill Volunteers" which plays bluegrass, gospel and country music at benefits, roasts, weddings and political functions. He also plays classical, jazz and dixie on the piano.

"He's good at it too," nods Peerless' friendly, freckled shop foreman, Don "Red" Triebold, the last of this family firm's second-generation employees.

In fact, Red remembers the company's early days when "we used to keep an old piano out in the shop, and Bruce used to wander back here anytime during the day and sit down and play it. He always played for all our Christmas parties too."

Although Bruce's body metronome constantly races in double time—and his lifestyle is definitely staccato—he somehow manages to keep the diverse rhythms of his work and his music in perfect harmony.

Just watch his excitement as he dashes out into his shop to take one more look at the gleaming stainless steel compressor that his firm is manufacturing for Armour and Co., Wilson Foods and Peer Food Products.

"It took us a year and a half to get all the bugs out," says this 5-foot 8-inch, 148-pound golfer with the pointed greying beard and mischievous brown eyes. . . .

Then catch Bruce's act later that night, when he's up on the stage with his musical partners Geoff Lutz and Worth Giller, tapping his feet, bobbing his head, and letting his fingers fly over the five-string guitar in a spritely rendition of "Country Roads" and then "Down by the Riverside."

It's just an intimate neighborhood party for 50 people, but Bruce, dressed in jeans, boots, open shirt and a red neckerchief, is giving it everything Judy Garland once gave Carnegie Hall.

And it becomes clear—watching Bruce move multo allegro in both places—that his life's composition flows smoothly because he enjoys everything so much. He always shoots for success, expects to find it, then greets it with delight.

He carries that optimism, expecting to win approval, with him, whether he's at home, in his office, in the shop, on a stage—or at a meeting of one of the several boards he serves on as a representative of small business.

In fact, his wife Janet, who he met when both were acting in the Oak Park Village Players in 1962, thinks Bruce sometimes carries his need to excel to a fault.

"Bruce likes to win and that's why he does. But he's not a good sport about losing," she says. "When we took up skiing as a family, our three children and I all came in with the first group in the beginning slalom race, and Bruce came in with the second. He tried to congratulate us, but it was hard for him because he really wasn't happy coming in second.

"Another time when we were visiting my brother and his wife in Alabama, we tried to play Scrabble, and we had to quit because my sister-in-law is so good. Bruce got so uptight when she won, he smashed his fist down on the table and yelled, 'Sandpail isn't a word!'"

But expecting to win is something that comes naturally to Bruce Petsche, because most of his life he has.

Born in Elmhurst, Bruce graduated from York High School, then sailed through Medill School of Journalism at Northwestern University,

EXHIBIT 13-2 (Continued)

picking up both bachelor's and master's degrees in advertising and marketing along the way.

At the same time, he worked part-time at the small Peerless Metal Fabricators Inc. that his 85-year-old father, a sheet metal worker, opened in 1946 at 3604 W. Chicago Ave. with a $10,000 savings account.

"From the beginning, we designed and built a variety of processing equipment for meat, food, pharmaceutical and manufacturing companies," Bruce explains, naming early customers the firm still has, such as Johnson & Johnson, Kraft Foods, the Kitchens of Sara Lee, R. R. Donnelly & Co., Cracker Jack and Borg-Warner. "I started to work here when I was 14. I never expected to make Peerless my career, but I never left."

He adds, somewhat abashedly, that his father always wanted the firm to remain small. Although admitting "sometimes I think he was right," Bruce was the driving force behind the expansion that finally drove the company to larger quarters in Bridgeview.

Yet all the time he's been working with Peerless Metal, Bruce always has been up on a stage somewhere in the evenings, making his name throughout the community as a composer and musician. . . .

Fulfilling his musical potential in recent years has meant entering the World's Greatest Ragtime Piano Player championship last year and the year before in Monticello. He won the first time, came in second the second—and he wasn't too thrilled about that.

Also, he and his partners in the Brush Hill Volunteers have been writing political satires, which they perform for League of Women Voters groups around the state; and Bruce recently wrote 18 sassy, snappy tunes for a "hit in the making" called "International Bernie," which was tried out at the Playwrights' Center in March, got good reviews and is shopping for producers.

Fulfilling his business potential has meant building—among other machinery—bigger and better "ham traps" and playing a tune on his company's bottom line.

Fulfilling his civic potential has meant serving on such boards as the Illinois Manufacturers' Assn., and several of its committees, including pollution control and its small business group.

He is an outspoken member of the state's employment security advisory board and he's been a strong voice against the Illinois Scaffold act, a law that's "been superseded by the workers comp act, but never has been repealed."

And Bruce labors around the clock, trying to resolve his "philosophical quagmire" regarding the steel workers union. "My grandfather was a charter member of the Cleveland chapter, my father always carried a union card, and I was a union musician for 15 years. I believe in everything they fought for, medical care, insurance, vacations—people deserve that. But just because they worked here five years, does that give them the right to take a two-hour job and stretch it to eight—and to increase wages until I'm paying a sheet metal worker $39,000?"

On the other hand, despite his tough talk, workers at Peerless Manufacturing know they have a loyal friend in Bruce Petsche.

"In June, when Local 73 went on strike a week, we were only out a few hours," puts in Red Triebold. "The next morning Bruce went down to the union hall, signed a pledge saying 'We'll agree to any terms you decide on, but I can't have my men out.' When he left, one of the union officials said, 'What this union needs is a negotiator like Bruce Petsche.' "

And Bruce fulfills himself as a Christian too, according to his friend and competitor Doug Venerka, head of Chicago Blow Pipe Co.

"I'll tell you a story that endeared Bruce to me forever," Doug begins. "He and I had known each other many years when my daughter Nancy came down with leukemia in 1977. We were alright financially, but Nancy needed something to think about, and she wanted a pony very much. So in order to keep her mind busy, Bruce took it upon himself to raise the money for a pony saddle among the business men in our community.

"We had to go live in Seattle, where Nancy was getting treatment, and at Christmas a big box arrived, and in it was the saddle. It was just what she needed—all that confusion, excitement and happiness. It was something that changed our lives.

"The end of the story is a happy one. Nancy not only survived and got that pony, but she is a healthy 14-year-old today. That's typical of Bruce, he gets on a cause and there's no stopping him."

Source: *Crain's Chicago Business*, Sept. 28, 1981, pp. 37–38.

when he had married, how many children he had, what his family life had been like, what his general lifestyle was.

Next we discussed business.

We talked about how the family business began, how it grew, how profits increased from the first year to the current one, how the staff had increased, what some of the major problems had been, who some of the biggest customers were in the beginning—and how many were still with him. We discussed his business philosophy (including his views on unions and moving from Illinois) and how his feelings had changed during the last few difficult years.

Then, we moved into the "other side" of this businessman's life that included his music and writing.

Deftly, Bruce Petsche outlined how his interest in music began and how it grew. Thoughtfully—and he claims for the first time—he talked about how important music had been in his life and how he developed an interest in it. We also talked about his partners in the band, how they're paid, and how he feels about that too.

Although I had plenty of material when we stopped talking that afternoon, it wasn't enough to start the story because the result would have been a "one-person" profile, and I wanted to find out what other people thought of him.

Before I arranged to meet him again—in his office-factory—I asked for the phone numbers of Petsche's wife, his top competitors, some people who served with him on the IMA, the musicians who played jazz with him, people who hired him to play for their parties, and some colleagues at his office and in the factory.

Now I had enough sources to begin work on my full feature.

By telephone from my office, I talked to all of those people and verified the facts given to me by Petsche—but they also revealed other dimensions of the man.

Each person saw another "side" of Bruce Petsche and told anecdotes to show me what he was really like and how it felt to live and work with him. I began to see the whole man—a sincere, caring person with a unique set of values.

But some negative traits emerged too. I saw that they too had to be included. The same force that drives the man to succeed in business and music can sometimes be irritating to those who love him and live with him.

In the course of those telephone calls, I also learned a good deal about the State of Illinois and its business problems.

When Bruce and I met the next time and I asked pointed questions about the union, he answered that he found himself in a peculiar dilemma. He represented management in negotiations and was the grandson of a founding member of the sheet metal workers' union.

During my visit, I saw him in his office, in the plant, and through the eyes of several people who work for him. I filled my bag with important information on, impressions of, and feelings about Bruce Petsche long before I began to write a tale about him.

Before starting to type, I read and reread my material, underlining and circling important facts, getting the central themes organized in my mind.

Then I asked myself:

- Why am I writing this story? What is the main point I want to make, to dispute, to illuminate?

- What are the four main impressions I'd like to leave with my readers about Bruce Petsche?

- Are there any contrasts or tensions that will create conflicts and different points of view in the story?

I went over the notes once more, with these three questions in mind, and an outline began to form. Like most writers, I carried the story around in my head a few days, repeating anecdotes, telling them to others, and trying to understand what made the man run so hard and so fast.

Realizing that Petsche was a fun-loving fellow, I thought the lead should be one that would make him—as well as the reader—smile.

Knowing he was a compassionate person, who has done many kind things for others, I plucked out anecdotes to use in key spots to keep reader interest up.

And realizing he's only human, I highlighted an amusing story that his wife told about his short temper when he is playing games.

Mix them all together and you have the profile about Bruce Petsche in Exhibit 13-1.

Remember, the press kit you prepare for your client or company should contain as many profiles as the subject justifies. For a new product introduction, use the company president, the director of manufacturing, and the head of research and development. For a new national advertising campaign, profile the product manager, the head of advertising, and a representative of the ad agency. Use your own judgment, but also use your imagination. Occasionally, it's a good idea to feature a minor functionary—a salesman or a factory worker—to get "the little guy's" point of view.

Although the profiles you write (or help write) should be geared primarily to "giving the facts," they should also be carefully and sensitively composed. Indeed, some stories, though not those usually done by publicists, must be written with the heart and hands of a poet, as was the portrait of photographer Victor Skrebneski by Henry Hanson, when he wrote for the *Chicago Daily News* (see Exhibit 13-2).

EXHIBIT 13-2. Profile: Victor Skrebneski.

Victor Skrebneski's world: A silver Mercedes under a dappled sycamore in a prize-winning yard

By Henry Hanson

High-fashion photography is a moist lip, a quicksilver mood—and maybe a navel. It is languorous beauty—captured in a flash. And gone.

It is Victor Skrebneski's world. Chicago's most successful fashion photographer, he's making international waves. And he creates in an incongruous setting.

Skrebneski's handsome studio-home on the Near North Side is sandwiched between a three-story walk-up home for ex-drug addicts who shave their heads and a Lutheran home for women with handicaps and emotional problems. Everyone seems to get along fine.

Skrebneski's lifestyle may be a cut above his neighbors'. But you'd expect that of a prominent photographer of long-stemmed beauties.

What is Skrebneski's world? It is . . .

A silver Mercedes parked under dappled sycamore trees lighted at night by floodlamps nestled amid ivy ground coverings in a prize-winning front yard.

"A sensuous celebration" of nudes—including actress Vanessa Redgrave ("wow, what a woman") and ballet's Dennis Wayne ("a friend of mine")—published in a book with Skrebnesli's blank-verse prolog. . . .

A magazine review trumpeted: "Cerebral as well as electric. Should end puritanism once and for all, but probably won't."

Photographing Orson Welles, Bette Davis, Andy Warhol and Liv Ullmann dressed in the same prop—a big, black turtle-neck sweater. "I must have bought it a hundred years ago at Brooks Brothers."

Jet travel to the West Coast to talk with literary agent Irving Lazar (who also is Richard M. Nixon's agent) about snapping Liza Minnelli, Katharine Hepburn, Dominique Sanda, Bette Midler and Barbra Streisand for a new Skrebneski book of photos.

Food: Chicago's Maxim's de Paris, New York's Veau d'Or, London's Guinea and Paris' Le Petit Montmorency.

Skrebneski is trying to set up a photo session with Jackie Onassis, who recently wrote for the *New Yorker's* "Talk of the Town" about the opening of the International Center for Photographs. No Jackie nudes. "She's an absolutely

EXHIBIT 13-2 (Continued)

beautiful woman. That's how she should be photographed," said Skrebneski.

Chicago magazine wants Skrebneski to shoot Mayor Daley for an issue on the city in the year 2000. Skrebneski has been warned that Daley "is very conscious about his jowls."

A small TV security camera peers down to screen callers buzzing the doorbell at the renovated Jalka family coachhouse, which is Skrebneski's studio-home.

With soft FM rock filtering Simon and Garfunkel's *My Little Town* from a speaker high in his white brick box studio, Skrebneski was finishing work on a sexy nude shot to publicize a new Broadway show—*Le Belly Button.* . . .

During an interview, Skrebneski served white wine on the rocks in Polish wine goblets. He chain-smoked Viceroy cigarets, which he stashes in the refrigerator near a dinner dish for his dog—a Shin-Tzu named "Shih-Tzu"—who likes pigs and has pig-of-the-month photographs taped on the wall over his bowl.

. . .On the walls are photos for ads that have sold millions of dollars worth of clothes (Marshall Field & Co.), cosmetics (Estee Lauder), cigarets (Virginia Slims), hair permanents (Toni) and LP record albums (Muddy Waters, Burt Bacharach, Lana Cantrell and Upchurch-Tennyson). . . .

His portraits cost $1,500: "People who want to be photographed nude should get it over with before they're 30. And first they must have a point of view about life."

He grew up at the foot of Rush St., son of a tool and die maker for International Harvester Co.

French films of Jean Cocteau at the old World Playhouse theater were a major childhood influence: "My father used to take me."

He buys his suits ($325 to $375) at New York's Denoyer Inc., which does not advertise.

His photos of Sen. George McGovern were auctioned for $2,500 each at a 1972 political fund raiser. He also has photographed Sheriff Richard Elrod.

He takes color with a Nikon camera, black and white with a Hasselblad and packs a pocket Canon 110 ED on vacations.

His woman models: "You've seen pictures in magazines of girls running, looking surprised, hair all blowing. My woman is not that wild, insane kind. She is . . . ladylike."

Nudes: "I photograph, design, make happen what I want to see: A statement—pure, simple, no tricks."

He dislikes photographing children and animals.

He admires Richard Avedon's work but felt Avedon's recent show at New York's Marlborough Gallery was badly designed. "Everything was white." He also likes Irving Penn, Helmut Newton and Horst, the Paris photograper who photographed Skrebneski's home for *House & Garden* last February.

He studied art at Roosevelt University and the Institute of Design of Illinois Institute of Technology, but is a self-taught photographer.

His pictures have been displayed at the Arts Club, Deson-Zaks Gallery and the now-shuttered Center for Photographic Arts on W. Erie, and he was honored in a multimedia event at the Museum of Contemporary Art.

Above his studio is a spacious apartment designed by interior designer Bruce Gregga. It is furnished with cubist art, 18th-century French furniture, a bronze by Max Ernst, sculpture by Man Ray, paintings by Gleizes, a Bombois nude and a Domela collage over the fireplace. "I like art of the '20s and '30s," said Skrebneski, who collects mostly in Paris and New York.

In the living room are three Lalanne fleece-lined sculptures of sheep—two headless and one with a head—that double for chairs.

In a parlor is a spindly floor lamp by Diego Giacometti. Under the parchment shade is a sculptured iron head resembling the heads of Skrebneski and his models—gaunt, unsmiling, world weary—but flattered by soft light from above.

Source: *Done in a Day* (Chicago: Swallow Press, 1977) pp. 147–150. © Field Enterprises, Inc.

Part IV

The Feature

Chapter 14

Developing a Topic

Now that you've conquered the inverted pyramid news story, learned how to get the most from an interview, and studied the profile, it's time to consider general feature writing—the ability to lend a little individualized, creative dash to your work.

While this special skill is generally regarded as the art form used in newspaper and magazine features, some of its basic techniques may be applied to all news stories, direct mail pieces, and press releases.

A good public relations counselor also understands all facets of the feature story so he or she can suggest story ideas to feature writers centering on his clients, recommend setting up interviews with everyone who may contribute information to the story, and offer graphic ideas for illustrating the story when it gets into print.

The same, of course, applies to broadcast journalism. The alert publicist is always keeping an eye out for settings that would look good on television—and at the same time put his client in front of a camera.

Actually there's much more to the public relations game than standard announcements of something new, like a promotion or acquisition or marketing plan. What your client needs most is the development of ongoing feature stories that will enhance his image and keep his name in the media in subtle ways.

Such stories will create a positive view of the things the corporation is doing and the ways in which your client or company is enriching society.

Once you understand the way feature stories are developed, you will automatically begin thinking in those terms. For example, the public relations woman handling a Chicago lawyer who had just set up a new law lab, which teaches people to become their own lawyers in simple procedures, had the good sense to call and tell me about the program.

She understood the ground rules of the newspaper at which I work. Our stories must be exclusive, or at least first; they must be about Chicago and about Chicagoans; and they must be of interest to the business community. Because her story satisfied all three criteria, we went ahead with the feature story. Since her client was a woman, she later suggested a feature story about her for *Working Woman* magazine and still later generated yet another story about her in the *Chicago Lawyer*, a local law newspaper.

There's also the possibility that you have enough talent and skill to learn to write your own feature stories in your spare time and sell them on a free-lance basis. Many public relations people do that and enjoy the material and intellectual benefits that the hobby brings to their lives.

Here's how to go about it, for either your own or your company's profit.

Think of feature-writing techniques as the frosting and trimming that will make your basic story more appealing to your reader.

Now, that doesn't mean you may write the story of Cinderella into your news report. You still have to stick to the facts.

But you may be able to add a little flavor—a dimension of personal thought and feeling—if you dig a little deeper, look a little closer, and listen a bit more carefully.

That's what feature writers always try to do.

There are some people who never become comfortable with feature stories but get the job done with a serviceable five-W news release. Others try to give their stories a feature lead almost every time. They do that because they think it's more fun to read a feature story and more fun to write one.

There's a personal, human element in feature writing that challenges the writer's imagination and enhances almost any story.

There are a variety of feature formulas that will help you bring this special touch to commonplace reports, either for press releases or media stories.

Regardless of which formula you choose, however, the first few sentences must give your reader a sense of what the story is going to be about and must play up its features, or most unusual aspect, in an interesting way.

A simple form to follow is to (1) block out the main themes you're going to emphasize and the quotes and anecdotes you have to support them and (2) outline them in diminishing importance, using transitional, explanatory paragraphs in between.

The transitional paragraphs are direct "reporting" that link the themes to each other. Follow each of those with either an anecdote or a quote that will reinforce its point.

Usually, a writer tries to save one of the strongest points (or transitional paragraphs) for the end of the feature and then follows it with an especially interesting, witty, or poignant quote or observation to provide the "snapper" finish.

An example of a thematic feature story is shown in Exhibit 14-1.

The first paragraphs establish the fact that suicides seem to be increasing among teens in suburbia. The following paragraphs bring in the theme that professionals agree, and statistics from a national survey are cited to prove that point.

The following theme consists of professionals' view of the most likely candidates for suicide. And the essay continues with a discussion of the causes and suggestions as to what parents may do to help prevent suicide.

The final theme, saved for the thought-provoking "snapper" finish, points out that there may be more suicides among the affluent because of less security and support. The child in the blue-collar home usually has the approval and encouragement of parents for every achievement. However, it may be more difficult for the child of a wealthy, highly educated, upward-striving family to feel the same way.

Sometimes, if you are writing a first-person story, for example, you may be able to skip the thematic approach and write the story in chronological order, as in the example shown in Exhibit 14-2.

EXHIBIT 14-1. A Thematic Feature Story.

Why too many execs' kids see suicide as a way out

By Sandra Pesmen

Three times in the past five years we have attended funerals for the children of friends.

One was a beautiful, talented 20-year-old college student from a greatly admired, achieving North Shore family. She had muscular dystrophy and was beginning to experience the debilitating effects of the disease.

She died after going into the garage, locking herself in the car and turning on the motor.

The second was a 17-year-old boy from a large family in which both parents were teachers. He was the only "problem child," burdened with a five-year history of delinquency, learning and drug problems.

He died from an overdose of pills.

The third was a 13-year-old. He was slim and frail and had four strong older brothers who excelled at sports and schoolwork.

He drowned in one of the three bathtubs in his $100,000 home.

On each of these occasions, in an effort to be kind, we, and most of the other bewildered, shocked and saddened attendees, spoke to the anguished parents in very guarded terms.

We referred to "the incident" and "the accident" when we extended our sympathies. . . .

Whether or not it is properly identified each time it occurs, it is suicide among the adolescent sons and daughters of Chicago's professionals and business executives. . . .

The National Institute of Mental Health reports suicide is the second leading killer of teenagers in the country, claiming almost 20,000 lives a year. Teen-age suicide has more than tripled since 1955. And although many incidents here are reported as accidents, north suburban officials still find New Trier Township statistics higher than the national average.

Some analysts believe the "contagion" stems from young people's strong sense of immortality, a belief that dramatic or dangerous activities somehow won't result in death. Experts also believe that some youngsters who witness suicide among peers or in the family begin to consider that as a feasible problem-solving mechanism. Statistics show that people who have a history of suicide in their families have a greater chance of committing it themselves.

Professionals define suicide as anger turned inward and the last, ultimate cry for help.

In the case of these particular teenagers and young adults, it's also a case of giving up because they don't feel they'll ever be able to meet the impossible goals set for them by their families.

"But it's the act of finally taking control, as well. They're trying to end depression and loneliness and feelings of inadequacy and low self-worth," explains Margery K. Fridstein, director of mental health and education for North Shore Mental Health Assn.'s Irene Josselyn Clinic.

Ms. Fridstein recalls that Chicago's elite began focusing on the problem three summers ago, after beautiful 18-year-old Rhonda Alter, daughter of a wealthy Highland Park real estate developer, drove her mother's sports car out to a park and hanged herself from a tree. At that time Rhonda's bewildered father described her as the "perfect" child, and no one seemed to know what made her do it.

Rumor had it that Rhonda killed herself because she hadn't been accepted to a prestigious college. Grist from that same mill also reported that Rhonda's acceptance notice arrived in the mail the day after her death.

With that kind of drama attached to it, suicide suddenly began to get more attention on the North Shore. Northfield police approached the North Shore Mental Health Assn. asking for help to educate the suburb's anxious public. At the same time, school administrators and clergymen began organizing public seminars on teenage suicide through the Jewish Family Services in Highland Park.

One of the most important messages to grow out of the studies, panels and seminars of that period was that one incident rarely is cause for a teen suicide.

"One event can trigger the action, but the problems that actually cause suicide by the affluent teenager develop over a long period of time," says Tema Rosenblum of Jewish Family Services.

"While the youngster may seem to commit the act to get attention, to punish a boyfriend or to make parents feel guilty, all suicides are some form of depression from which the victim can see no relief."

And where does such destructive depression come from in this affluent promised land, and why do its victims take such drastic measures against it?

According to Ms. Rosenblum, it begins with the individual's feelings of low esteem that are an outgrowth of failure to meet his or her parents' expectations.

These particular families move to large, lovely homes in neighborhoods that have good schools. Then they work hard to earn enough money to pay for them, because they want to give their children pleasant, beautiful, perfect surroundings.

They're striving to seem perfect, she adds, and to have perfect children, to reenforce their own faltering sense of worth.

"They're successful, high-aspiring, affluent, competitive, accomplished—and want their children to be all of those things, too," explains therapist Rosenblum.

So these basically insecure parents push, protect, plan and arrange for their children to be successful

EXHIBIT 14-1 (Continued)

and accepted by their peers—wrongly stressing *external* values—what the kids wear and how well they perform—rather than the children themselves.

"I counsel pregnant women who ask the names of the best nursery schools, so their unborn child will have a head start in kindergarten, in order to do well in grade school, which should help them in high school so they can get to the best colleges," Ms. Rosenblum continues. "Granted, some kids flourish in that kind of atmosphere, but we can't forget that some very adequate, very average kids can't live up to those kinds of expectations, and they become more and more depressed and eventually give up."

The parents of one youngster who committed suicide two years ago still can't understand why it happened. They were very devoted to all their children, and after noticing this boy's problems in early adolescence, they went with him to counseling. As the psychiatrists' bills mounted, this pair continued to do their best to help their son feel loved and to build up his self-esteem—even to the point of selling their home and buying a smaller one so they could continue his therapy.

"We always had a peaceful, happy home; we always worked hard and spent a good deal of time with all the children," recalls the father, a successful attorney. His wife, popular with her peers as well as active in school, church and civic affairs, doesn't understand what happened either.

But therapists believe that the couple's perfection was what depressed their son most. "When parents put forth perfection as a model, the child is overwhelmed by their omnipotence," explains Ms. Rosenblum. "And as he grows older, if he never sees his parents make any mistakes, he begins to feel he'll never be able to live up to their expectations for him. It also instills fears in him about separating from this family, which has made life so beautiful for him. He begins to suspect he won't be able to provide all of those external comforts and perfections by himself."

A child from a home of less perfection and achievement doesn't have to work as hard to gain sincere approval from his parents. That child is greeted with wonder, approval—even cheers—whenever he or she does anything of merit. Graduation from each public school level is cause for great pride and celebration.

"The child in the blue-collar home walks with the confidence that when he or she leaves his house of origin, he or she can do as well or better than his or her parents, and win their approval and admiration," Ms. Rosenblum remarks. "Can the wealthy teenager of the successful chief executive officer say the same?"

Searching for symptoms and help

How can you tell if a young person may be contemplating suicide? Here are a few symptoms to watch for:

- Declining school performance coupled with expressions of apathy and helplessness. This might include a sudden loss of interest in sports, hobbies or organizations that previously had been a source of pleasure for the person.
- The recent loss of a loved one, particularly someone in the family.
- Changes in eating or sleeping habits that may mask deep internal feelings of depression.
- Direct suicide threats such as "I wish I were dead" or "I have nothing to live for."
- Family disruptions and crises such as divorce, critical illness of a family member, family relocation and loss of employment of one or both parents.
- Evidence that the teenager is being disparaged at home—when he or she is not communicating or is feeling alienated from his or her family.
- An absence of normal social contacts. This might include wanting to spend excessive amounts of time alone as well as a noticeable withdrawal from family and friends.
- Patterns of impulsiveness or excess: taking risks or dares, abusing alcohol or drugs, unusual outbursts of temper, i.e., a general lack of concern for personal safety or strong feelings of guilt over the smallest mistake or failure.
- Getting rid of possessions.

How can you help in a suicidal crisis?
- Recognize the clues.
- Trust your judgment. Don't let others convince you to ignore clues.
- Tell others. You may have to betray a confidence.
- Stay with a suicidal person until help arrives or a crisis passes.
- Listen intelligently—encourage the suicidal person to talk to you.
- Urge professional help. Encourage the person to seek help from a therapist during the crisis or after an attempt.
- Be supportive. Show the person you care and help the person feel worthwhile and wanted.

Some numbers to call for help are:
Evanston Hospital Crisis Intervention (24 hours)—**492-6500**
Irene Josselyn Clinic (daytime)—**441-5600**
Metro-Help—**929-5150**
Family Service Center (24 hours)—**251-7350**
Jewish Family Service—**831-4225**

Source: *Crain's Chicago Business*, Nov. 2, 1981, pp. 49–50.

EXHIBIT 14-2. A Chronological Feature Story

Searching for the perfect door is not an open-and-shut case

By Bob Zeni

Renovating your house? Need a door? Going to buy a door? Have fun.

My wife Wendy and I were renovating our living room last summer and we needed a new front door. The lock was shot and the door was warped, leaking cold air in winter and yet fitting so tightly that it would open only with the application of battering-ram force. We thought it a bit much to ask our dinner guests to wear shoulder pads.

It seemed so simple. Just go to the lumber yard and buy a door. So one evening in mid-June we set out for Gee Lumber in La Grange. On our way out, we measured the door. It turned out to be 33½ inches by 79½ inches, slightly smaller than 34 by 80 (or in door lingo, two-ten by six-eight).

Gee didn't carry doors in the size or style to match our Georgian home. But they would gladly order one for us. We flipped through their catalog and found the right style.

"We'd like this one."

"Can't get that one in a two-ten by six-eight."

What if we bought the larger size and cut it down to fit the doorway?"

"I wouldn't do that if I were you! These doors are filled with wood chips. You cut too much, and the chips'll pour out the door."

I looked at Wendy. In her eyes I saw the living room carpeting, freshly shampooed and covered with a three-inch layer of sawdust. I also saw myself behind a vacuum cleaner trying to clean up a three-inch layer of sawdust.

We canvassed our friends. One suggested a place called Pic-A-Dor at 5340 W. 111th in Oak Lawn. We drove 30 minutes to get there only to find that it wasn't open that night. The next week, we tried again with more success.

The selection at Pic-A-Dor included doors with circular windows; square windows; pentagonal, hexagonal, octagonal windows; with a series of three rectangular windows arrayed on a diagonal. In short, every door imaginable.

Except a two-ten by six-eight Georgian.

The proprietor showed us a catalog—no luck—and then offered to manufacture a door that *looked* Georgian by mounting molding on a flush door.

I thought of that for a moment until I turned to my wife. Now, Wendy has very expressive eyes and after several years of marriage, I've found that I need not ask her opinion because she will give it to me without speaking.

I declined the proprietor's offer.

Sick of driving around, I let my fingers do the walking. Ads in the Yellow Pages told us of garage doors, aluminum doors, screen doors, storm doors and even steel doors "with the beautiful *look* of wood." It was enough to give me a hangnail. . . .

Maybe there were alternatives. We could buy a Georgian in one of the standard sizes. We could enlarge the doorway, but that would mean cutting through bricks. Or we could reduce the size of the doorway, but that would mean matching the color of the new brick to the color of the old brick. I was having enough trouble finding a door; who wanted to go out looking for bricks?

A friend suggested Salvage One, which boasts that it carries 17,000 doors. We looked at all 17,000 and found three two-tens by six-eights. One was missing a 6-square-inch chunk. One was a quarter-inch too wide and the third was fitted with a piece of beautifully etched glass—an open invitation to neighborhood vandals.

So we gave up.

What the hell, we'll buy a new lock, weatherstrip and have a carpenter plane the reluctance off the top, sides and bottom.

Back to Pic-A-Dor

So, back to Pic-A-Dor in late July to invest $80 in a top-of-the-line lock and deadbolt set.

Several days later, the carpenter arrived. He pulled off the old lock and took one look.

"This new one won't fit."

"What?"

EXHIBIT 14-2 (Continued)

It seems the old lock had replaced an even older one. The person who put in that one (may he be condemned to spend eternity opening doors that open only to more doors) made it fit by stuffing wood putty all around it. Wood putty that crumbled and wouldn't support a new lock.

Wonderful. An $80 lock and no door to put it on.

But the carpenter had seen a freshly made door at an Edward Hines lumber yard in La Grange, not five minutes from our house.

So the next Saturday, Wendy and I visited Edward Hines. We asked the gentleman behind the desk how we order a door.

"We don't make doors."

"Our carpenter was here two days ago and he said you make doors. In fact, he said there's one sitting out in the yard."

"He's wrong."

Pulling my hair out

If I had allowed myself the pleasure of pulling my hair out, I would have been bald within minutes. Wendy and I walked out into the yard, found the door and asked a passing employee (pencil tucked behind ear, overalls, sawdust in eyebrows), "Edward Hines make doors?"

"Yeah, I ordered that one."

I tackled the yardman and dragged him into the office to introduce him to the deskman. I pointed at the yardman.

"This man ordered the door that Edward Hines made that's sitting out in the yard."

"We don't make doors."

"Sure we make doors."

"Since when?"

"I don't know. I think we've always made 'em."

The yardman walked behind the desk and handed me a catalog.

I looked at Wendy. In her eyes I saw the headlines: MAN RUNS AMOK, KILLS TWO WITH CATALOG. I saw her visiting me in a

cell made entirely of padded doors, each one secured with one of those $80 locks.

But, amidst desperation, here was hope. We paged through it. I trembled in anticipation. There, a two-ten by six-eight in the right style.

Ours for $250.

What to do, what to do. Do we spend $250 to have a door made for us? Or do we save the money and use the $80 lock as a paperweight? Well, I wasn't going to waste the entire summer and end up with the same damn door I started with.

So on Aug. 1 we plunked down a $150 deposit. Then we waited. And waited. And waited.

Two months later, on Oct. 2, it arrived. I gave them the other $119.07 (taxes, you know) and spent the next Saturday lovingly sanding it. I rubbed it to remove the dust. I stained one side. The next day, I painted the other side with exterior paint.

Then I waited for it to dry. And waited. And waited.

Paint doesn't dry when the weather turns cool, and last October, as I well remember, it was not only cool, it was conspiratorially cold.

Three weeks later, on Oct. 29, the carpenter returned.

There were problems, of course. I had bought hinges with rounded corners to replace the old hinges that had squared-off corners. And the carpenter spent nearly three hours installing the lock—those top-of-the-line models are complicated.

But finally, it worked. At long last, after nearly six months of looking for one, our house had a new door. Not counting traveling expenses, it cost $560.63.

But was it worth it?

Was it worth the disappointment, the anger, the fatigue, the frustration and the thoughts of homicide?

Hell, no.

It still leaks cold air in the winter.

Source: *Crain's Chicago Business,* Feb. 15, 1982, pp. 37–38.

EXERCISE 14-1

Following is a feature story by *Chicago Sun-Times* Pulitzer Prize-winner Mike Royko.

Read it carefully. Then identify component parts of it, naming: (1) the lead, (2) the main themes, (3) the transitional paragraphs, anecdotes, quotes and explanations, and (4) the snapper finish.

What news announcement made this feature timely?

'When you are eatin' regular, what is a Great Lake or two?'

By Mike Royko

When I was a kid, the best days of the summer were spent at the beach.

The cinder-covered schoolyard was too hot and dusty for softball. The alleys were so choked with flies and garbage smells that hunting bottles for their 2-cent deposits was no fun.

So we grabbed our itchy wool trunks, a fried-egg sandwich, rode a North Ave. streetcar to the end of the line, and there it was—the big, blue, cool, clean lake.

You could smell it and taste it long before you saw it.

We threw our bony bodies at the waves, sprawled on the sand, stared in boyish awe at the older girls and went home exhausted, bleached and ready for 10 hours of deep sleep.

Sometimes we went to fish. I was lucky because the local tavern gentlemen didn't mind taking a kid along. Tiny the fat man, Chizel and Clem were good conversationalists as well as fine fishermen.

They sat for hours on the rocks, muzzling bottles of cold beer, talking about the Cubs' pennant chances (a long time ago) and pulling fat, needle-boned perch from the lake with their bamboo poles.

So I like the lake. I like knowing that Indians used it, city kids used it and hundreds of thousands of people still use it.

And I get sick and angry when I hear someone like Thomas H. Coulter, chief executive officer of the Chicago Assn. of Commerce and Industry, say:

"Our lakefront is not much more than a wasteland. Oh, it has some trees, but the only time I've been on the lakefront in the last 30 years has been to McCormick Place.

"I'm sure that is true of the 20 million other persons who have gone to McCormick Place, not so much for commercial or business meetings of various kinds, but for cultural programs, art, theater, ballet. . . ."

As a newspaperman, I've had to listen to some odd ideas—from Skid Row winos, aldermen, singing mice and editors—but I've heard nothing to compare with Coulter's blather.

He was making a pitch for further expansion of McCormick Place, the Tribune's grotesque Temple of $$$.

Coulter is paid to say things like that. He works for and with the city's commercial and business interests.

But even from a paid mouthpiece, it was in bad taste. His rich crowd has misused the beautiful lake. And a gentleman doesn't speak badly of a lady he has misused.

The lakefront is not yet a wasteland, despite what Coulter says. But it is on its way. And who has caused it?

When I went swimming, I took a shower in the bathhouse and left the lake as clean as I found it. When we caught fish, we took what we wanted to eat.

Ah, but what of Coulter's employers—the rich, smoke-belching industrial fat cats? They've poured enough slop into the lake to make a million pigs sick.

They've stunted and killed the fish and are rapidly making most of the shoreline unfit for humans. Beaches on the Far South Side and in Indiana have become sewers. Thank you, commerce and industry.

And the view from the shoreline? The swimmers, cyclists, fishermen, picnickers and golfers didn't blot it out. But the real-estate interests are crawling to the water's edge for their rich high-rise profits.

A wasteland? Not yet, but some day it will be. And it won't matter a bit to the commerce-and-industry crowd. They have their spacious suburban surroundings, their back-yard and country-club pools and their summer homes.

They don't use the lakefront except for yachting. So they dispatch a handsome, manicured, Canadian-born, Pennsylvania-educated suburbanite to inform us that it is a wasteland.

He probably thinks it is, because he doesn't go there to see the hundreds of thousands of ordinary yahoos using the beaches, parks and paths.

From the patio, one can't see that the lakefront is draped with humanity from Foster Av. to the Far South Side on warm weekends.

Oh, it is true that many of the users—especially south of McCormick Place—are Negroes. But even the most ignorant or the richest bigot shouldn't kill a lake because Negroes are dipping their toes in it. Yet a red-nosed politician once told me: "I don't care what happens to Jackson Park. Niggers have took it over."

The "lake-is-a-wasteland" people have wonderful arguments. Remember, they are doing something noble while pouring industrial wastes into the water and gobbling up the shoreline. They EMPLOY people. They put food in our mouths, clothes on our backs, roofs over our heads. So when you are eatin' regular, what is a Great Lake or two?

Spare me that soul talk. They employ people so their companies profit and they can make $70,000 a year plus stock options and early retirement plans.

And living the good life is worth the price of creating a concrete-walled septic tank bordered by four states.

Putting McCormick Place on the lake was a mistake. Expanding it is a mistake.

It should have been built in Cicero or on Rush St. That's where the action is. Conventioneers aren't looking for sunshine or moonlight glittering on the water. Ask the vice cops.

But it is there and the people who put it there are committed to it. And if they say the lakefront is a wasteland, they must be right. And they will do everything they can to prove they are right—including making it a wasteland.

Source: *Done in a Day*, pp. 40–42. © Field Enterprises, Inc.

Chapter 15

Finding the Lead

If you want to add dash to a routine story, try beginning with something other than a straight five-W lead. Use

- A quotation

- A question

- A summary statement

- An anecdote

- An example

- A description

With some practice, you'll find it's easy to apply these forms to breaking news; company announcements of promotions, new products, and expansions; and reports of meetings, conventions, and speeches.

A glance through almost any paper will show you quickly that most professionals try to use feature leads with regularity. Their attraction is that the heart of any feature story is human interest, built on passion and pathos.

In a news report of a man who died while trying to rescue his son from their burning home, reporter Hanke Gratteau of the *Chicago Sun-Times* used the quotation feature lead:

"We thought this year would be better," said the tearful wife of a Wood Dale man who died Sunday as he unsuccessfully tried to rescue a son from their burning home.

Her husband, Wilbur Gibson, 44, and son, Thomas, 19, died apparently of smoke inhalation in a fire that broke out early Sunday morning in their home at 314 N. Ash. They were pronounced dead at Alexian Brothers Medical Center, Elk Grove Village.

Gibson, his wife, Vivian, and another son, Jeffrey, 16, had fled the burning second-floor bedrooms to the safety of the first floor when they heard Thomas' screams for help.

"I don't know if he had locked his door," said Mrs. Gibson, 37, "or if he was panicky. But we heard him screaming for someone to go up and help him. My husband wet down a blanket and went up the stairs. And neither one came down."

Jeffrey was lying in bed listening to music when he smelled smoke, Mrs. Gibson said.

"There must have been a spark from a plug that hit his mattress. He threw water on it, but he couldn't put it out. That's when he woke us up," she said.

The family was plagued by health and financial problems last year. Gibson, a maintenance supervisor for an Elk Grove company, recently had returned to work

115

after a three-month strike. Mrs. Gibson has a heart condition and was hospitalized several times last summer.

"We thought this year was going to be better," she said Sunday. "And now. . . ."

After being treated for minor injuries, Mrs. Gibson and Jeffrey were staying with relatives in Roselle. She said she doubted they would return to the Wood Dale home.

Neighbors have established an emergency fund for the family at Elmhurst Savings & Loan in Wood Dale.

Funeral services will be held at 11 a.m. Wednesday at Gells Funeral Home, 180 S. York Rd., Bensenville. Burial will be in Arlington Cemetery, Elmhurst. Visitation will be from 2 to 9:30 p.m. Tuesday at the funeral home.

On Saturday, a 94-year-old woman died when fire destroyed her Lemont Township home.

Ann Goode, who lived alone at 125 Archer, was dead on arrival at Palos Community Hospital, a hospital spokesman said.

Cook County sheriff's police found the single-story home engulfed in flames while on routine patrol. After firemen from Lemont aided by two other departments extinguished the flames, the woman's body was found in the rubble.

Police Sunday were trying to determine the cause of the fire.

Another excellent quote lead appeared in a recent story about tapes revealing that Franklin Delano Roosevelt got a warning from the Japanese before the December 7, 1941, bombing of Pearl Harbor. The Chicago Tribune Press Service story began:

"God!" the man said, "That's the first time any damned Jap has told us to get out of Hawaii. And that has me more worried than any other thing in the world. . . ."

The date was Oct. 8, 1940. The place was the Oval Office of the White House and the man was President Franklin D. Roosevelt, speaking into a recording device he had probably forgotten about.

A question lead was used by Jack Schnedler, now travel editor for the Chicago Sun-Times, when he interviewed author Joseph Heller for the Chicago Daily News. Because Heller had written his first book in 1962 and his second in 1974, Schnedler asked:

Tell us, Joe, why do you write so slow?
"Because I can't do it any quicker," says Joseph Heller, in a voice that unmistakably grew up around New York's Coney Island.

On the editorial page of the Chicago Tribune, writer Joan Beck began a story about the influence of genes on crime with the question lead:

Are some children born with the genetic bent to commit crime? Can criminals—citing scientific evidence—blame their genes for behavior which the law yolds is their personal responsibility? Is the discredited old "bad seed" theory going to be recycled again?

Summation leads are among the most provocative, for they quickly—and cleverly—sum up the meaning of the whole story in one phrase. They give the reader the essence of what the whole picture is. This is often the most difficult—as well as the most effective—way to begin a story.

Ellen Warren, Washington correspondent for the Chicago Sun-Times is a master of the summary lead. She wrote one of her classics the night she was sent to cover the arrival of Olga Korbet, Russian Olympic medalist, at O'Hare.

Watching the tiny athlete walk through the throngs crowding the airport, Warren came up with "The pigtails stood out like wild daisies," and everybody knew exactly who she was writing about, for the pigtails had become Olga's international trademark.

Lee Kottke, a feature writer for the now-defunct Chicago Daily News, once began a series about violent children with "Some kids could kill you—and they do."

I remember writing a series about women who became mothers after 40 and using this summary lead: "She has hot flashes, crinkles at the corners of her blue eyes, grey hair—and two-year-old-twins.''

On another occasion I interviewed a Miss America who insisted she didn't care anything at all about the large money prize, but was simply patriotic about her title. That interview became sillier and sillier, until I was moved to write the summary lead, "Miss America has lots of dollars—but very little sense."

June Kronholz, of the *Wall Street Journal* began a story about Namibia with this anecdote:

> On a still, moon-bathed evening, the South African army aimlessly lobs mortar shells into the desert a few miles south of the Angolan border. No one answers the guns; no one ever fires back.
>
> It is a nightly routine here in South Africa's war zone with the Namibian guerrillas. It reminds anyone listening that despite a decade of bush war, South Africa still rules Namibia.

A story in *USA Today* by Karen Heller began with the following anecdote:

> Erica Pressman is a young woman of infinite taste and wisdom, someone who knows what she likes and how to get it. No fashion sloth she, Erica knows her Calvins from her Vanderbilts, her Levi's from her personal favorite, Jordache.
>
> "I like Jordache because Jordache has the look that's right," says the Pikesville, Md., native as she strolls through Bamberger's designer clothing department at Hunt Valley Mall near Baltimore.
>
> Erica, resplendent in her tight-fitting denims, is 5 years old.

Karen Peterson, also of *USA Today*, begins a feature story with an example that reads:

> The women are "faithful, devoted, unspoiled and loving," says the catalog. They're women like 20-year-old Rebecca from the Philippines, 5 feet 4 inches tall, 110 pounds, who likes "cooking, collecting stamps and sight seeing."
>
> And would like to marry an American.

That kind of pitch is working for "mail-order-bride" companies capitalizing on what they see as wreckage from the women's liberation movement—disillusioned men seeking the stereotype of the subservient Asian wife.

Burt Schorr and Timothy D. Schellhardt used the following example lead in a *Wall Street Journal* story about the effect of Reagan budget cuts on Hartford's poor and middle class:

> Hartford, Conn.—Last October, President Reagan's first budget-reduction blitz sent hardly a ripple through the lives of Carmen Fernandez, Raquel Thompson and Catherine Maye.
>
> Mrs. Fernandez was enjoying her job at the Federal fuel-assistance office here. Mrs. Thompson's bilingual-education classes of 15 to 20 students had gotten off to a good start at Hartford high school and Mrs. Maye had qualified for a federal rent subsidy for herself and her retarded daughter.
>
> But now, a year later, the three women find themselves victims of the federal scythe.

Some of the finest feature leads of all kinds are collected in a book called *Done in a Day*, 100 years of great writing from the *Chicago Daily News*, published by the Swallow Press, Inc., shortly before the demise of that newspaper.

Any serious student of feature writing should have a copy. The best way to write good feature stories is to read them, for both pleasure and profit. Since this collection includes many of the best in the business, there is much to be learned from reading it.

Almost every lead in the book will knock your socks off.

For example, award-winning special writer M. W. Newman uses the following descriptive lead to report the record-breaking, 23-inch snowfall that hit Chicago in 1967:

> It came walloping over the plains like a swollen fist, scooped up all of Chicago and casually tangled it in knots.
>
> The stricken metropolis lay gasping, barely able to move.
>
> The storm swatted it, slugged it,

smashed it, crushed it in 75 million tons of snow.

But in the end, the metropolis did not break. Like a dazed giant, it shuddered under the monstrous weight and began stumbling to its knees . . . then regained its feet.

In April 1967, when Chicago had its worst tornado disaster, that same writer was assigned to cover it. Gathering his facts, observing that there were 54 dead, 1,975 injured, and $50 million in property damage, Newman wound up and wrote:

On a perfect day for tornadoes, the sky fell in.

Death came dancing and skipping, whistling and screaming, strangely still one second and whooshing and bouncing the next.

For some in the Chicago area, death was a black cloud funnel, toeing the earth and crushing the skulls of children.

Most news stories in *Done in a Day* display descriptive, example, anecdotal, or summary leads, but they all make sure to get the five Ws woven in at the top of the story, even if they don't come in standard one- or two-sentence form.

Generally, the inverted pyramid form discussed in the chapter on newswriting is always used. However, the feature writer often tries to wrap his story up with what is called a "snapper" finish—a quip or an anecdote. That makes it necessary to trim the stories more carefully than one trims an inverted pyramid news story.

With these examples in mind, you should be able to take an ordinary set of facts and turn them into a report using one of these feature-story leads.

Using the feature-story devices discussed in this chapter, write a news release for each of the items in Exercises 15-1, 15-2, and 15-3.

EXERCISE 15-1

The Continental Restaurant in the lobby of the Arlington Park Hilton, called Dunton's, will serve a special supper Friday, February 12 and Saturday, February 13. The dinner, called "Sweetheart Dinners for Two," will be priced at $35.

Anyone who comes to the Valentine's Day dinner will receive complimentary passes to the Cinderella Rockefella nightclub next door. The hotel is at 3400 W. Euclid Avenue, in Arlington Heights, Illinois. For reservations call 394-2000.

EXERCISE 15-2

Write a news release based on the following information.

The Alumni Association of Lake Forest School of Management will present a program on January 25 at 7:00 P.M. It will be held in the college, and featured speaker will be Herbert E. Neil, Jr., vice president of Harris Trust and Savings Bank and chairman of the Investment Strategy Committee for the bank. He will discuss the meaning of Reaganomics, explain the difference between it and other economic theories, and forecast its possibility for success.The talk is called "Will Reaganomics Work?" For information call 234-5005.

EXERCISE 15-3

Write a news release from the following facts.

> The Chicago Historical Society will sponsor a two-hour program for children ages 7–12 on Saturday, January 30, at 10:00 A.M. and again at 1:00 P.M. The program is a special workshop on the sports and games of America's past. It is called "Games People Played" and costs $3.00 per child and $2.00 for members of the society. For information call 642-4600. The Society is at Clark Street at North Avenue, Chicago.
>
> The workshop will include "Count Coup" and "Stare Eyes," Native American games that developed skills needed in tribal warfare and hunting. Kids will also take part in "Americans and English," a tug of war that children played during the American Revolution.

Chapter 16

Writing a Feature

Until now, we've been considering news stories and news feature articles written as the news breaks. There are some reporters who will never be content to write anything else.

I remember once talking about that with Ellen Warren, of the *Chicago Sun-Times,* when we both were working for the *Chicago Daily News.*

I was in the middle of a long feature story when we met at the coffee machine. Ellen was complaining that she was bored because it was a slow day on the city desk—nothing was happening.

I asked why she didn't switch to the features department, since she certainly had the wit, imagination, and style necessary for the job. Ellen smiled, shook her head, and said: "Even though this gets boring once in a while when nothing is happening, it's much more exciting to report news. I think it's the immediacy that makes it fun."

Feature writers thrive on just the opposite. The things they write about are rarely happening at that moment; so it's unusual for them to tell the world something newsworthy before anybody else has.

That's why they're of special value to publicists who need to keep telling their clients' stories in new ways.

The challenge is to take an incident that's already occurred, find a special approach through some new, undisclosed development, and turn the story around, using the special angle as the focus.

In other words, feature writers specialize in turning olds into news. They dress it up and bring out aspects everyone else has overlooked. And that is often the most important job of a public relations consultant too.

Of course, it helps to know all the different kinds of feature stories. You must also be aware of:

- Where they come from

- How you may help editors and reporters develop them

- To whom you can suggest them

- How you may assist writers so they'll be encouraged to pursue them. (Most feature stories, if they're to succeed, take even more research, planning, time, and thought than covering a news event does.)

In other words, the five-W news story immediately tells the reader what he must know about the event. But the feature story comes along later, with additional information and told in a different, in-depth, and more interesting way. That's the kind of ink that keeps your client in the limelight.

Examples of the different kinds of stories can be seen in the PR work done for the 100th anniversary of the Chicago Institute for Psychoanalysis in 1982. The public relations consultant at the Public Relations Board sent a folder containing the announcement and background information to all the media people, and some picked the story up as a small news item. During the year-long celebration, however, the Public Relations Board worked to keep a positive image of the Institute and its birthday before the public.

The Board took the first step by placing an extensive in-depth story tracing 50 years of psychoanalysis at the Institute in an excellent article in the *Chicago Tribune Sunday Magazine.* The story, written by Robert Cross and called "Inside Chicago's Shrink Factory," explained how, for 50 years, the Midwest's leading school of psychoanalysis "has been raising eyebrows and man's unconscious."

During that same period, the feature section of *Crain's Chicago Business* took still another approach.

Since *CCB* readers are business people, and one of the most important contributions the Institute has made is insight into the effect of death, I wrote a story about the impact of a death in the office on other workers. After interviewing George Pollock, psychoanalyst at the Institute who has studied the problem, I learned, "Death doesn't go away simply because the service is over and the boss says it's time to get back to work. Death in the office inspires as much prolonged sorrow as a death in the family."

These examples should help you think of varied ways to develop feature stories from one news item that you can suggest for newspaper feature sections, special publications, television and radio feature shorts, and weekly community and trade papers, as well as magazines.

Try to think of the feature story as an opportunity for you to paint an entire picture slowly, in full color, with lots of space and magnificent oils—as opposed to the small, black and white Instamatic photo that a news reporter is forced to create on deadline.

But before you get too carried away with the idea of "creative" writing, keep in mind—and

avoid—what I call "The Jimmy's World Temptation."

That happens when a reporter makes an effort to create an especially interesting feature but doesn't bother to get the facts. That's never allowed—and always unforgiveable.

But it happened when *Washington Post* feature writer Janet Cooke wrote a story about child heroin addicts—without having enough facts. She wrote the story anyway, creating dramatic and very effective scenes in her imagination and passing them off as truth in a story called "Jimmy's World."

The truth became public after Ms. Cooke received a Pulitzer Prize for her efforts—which her embarrassed newspaper later returned.

The lesson here is that although imagination and creativity can help make feature stories more interesting, one must never allow fiction to play any role in any form of journalism.

As with any story, begin by sitting down with your notes and thinking about what it is you want to say. Next, list the four most important things you want your reader to know about your subject. Try and let those four themes dominate the first outline for your story.

It's also important to ask the people who contribute information to agree to attribution. Stories are always more believable when the sources are clearly identified, rather than quoted as "spokesmen" and "observers."

And that brings us to a new trend in feature writing—Judgmental Journalism.

Until the late 1960s, most journalists agreed that every fact had to be presented objectively, with both sides of each story presented fairly, leaving the final judgment to the reader.

In those days, reporters joked about breaking the "I" on the typewriters of egotistical reporters who dared to use it regularly. Even most columnists went out of their way to write "this reporter" instead of "I" in an effort to appear more professional and detached.

Then, the 1970s drove us into the "Me Generation," and with it came "I journalism." Suddenly reporters all over the country started their stories with leads like this one: "I am standing here in the dark and I am tired. There are sounds of night around me." And the focus turned, more often than not, away from the news story and toward the "personality reporter."

Like most trends, "I journalism" finally diminished. Most reporters now make fairly conservative use of the first person, using it less often but in a more natural and effective way.

As a result of that trend, however, readers have come to expect some subtle inclusion of the writer's opinion in feature stories. As an image builder, you must be aware that the reporter will have some feelings about your client and will be ready to make some judgments about the company. Always consider the pros and cons the reporter may want to develop and help your client deal with them before the interview.

EXERCISE 16-1

Visit a retail store in your neighborhood. Talk with the owner to gather information for three different stories:

1. Write a short news report of his newest marketing strategy.

2. Write a longer news story describing that strategy but including feature elements of the shop that it will involve.

3. Write a feature profile about the owner of the shop.

Chapter 17

Choosing an Approach

There are several different kinds of feature stories that will give you an opportunity to use your literary virtuosity:

- Trend stories
- Service pieces
- Essays
- Contests

The most timely feature stories are those that reflect trends—interests, moods, and activities that are moving across the city or country and affecting the lives of your readers.

As I stressed early in this book, journalism is not a profession for people who cut themselves off from society. In order to succeed at the job, you must be involved in your community, as well as sensitive to the needs, problems, and joys of the people in it. You must be able to feel their changing moods and have the chutzpah to get out there in the trenches and ask them how and why the trends affect them.

So, it's only natural that most publicists as well as reporters get their best story ideas from friends, relatives, colleagues, and neighbors—all the people with whom they come into contact.

I walk about the city in which I work and the suburb in which I live listening very carefully to small talk. The offhand comments I hear often lead to interesting trends that develop into feature stories. I count time spent on my commuter train vital research. It's certainly proven fruitful in developing contacts, sources, and story ideas.

For example, one morning a neighbor friend who rides downtown with me commented that an interior decorator wanted $200 to make a circular dropcloth for a small table in his living room. This man, a 48-year-old insurance broker, was infuriated, so he went to the Singer Sewing Company, rented a machine, took some lessons, and made the cloth himself. He returned for more lessons and eventually bought the machine and made draperies to match the cloth. Now he does all the family mending, but his wife doesn't like him to tell anyone because she's concerned it will give him a "feminine" image.

While he was confessing all this to me, another male neighbor leaned over from across the aisle and said, "Say, that's silly—I sew too. We went out to price cloths for our new dining room set, and they were so outrageous, I bought linen and made them myself."

Obviously, there was a trend here to pursue. (It would have been nice if the sewing machine companies' PR people had found it.)

My first calls were to several sewing machine centers where instructors informed me they had seen an increase in the number of males in their sewing classes during the last four years. In a form of reverse liberation, men had begun to enjoy this creative and economical hobby, they assured me.

My next effort was to find more men to talk to me about their experiences. I located them by contacting the sewing teachers in several neighborhoods and following up the leads they gave me. I admit that three of the men I called hung up on me and asked me not to mention them in my story. I respected their feelings, of course, and still managed to come up with the feature shown in Exhibit 17-1.

On another occasion, I noted a trend that I felt needed investigation. We had just begun our newspaper's "Datebook," a listing of important business seminars and workshops held in the city each week.

As I began to compile the listings, I soon noticed an abundance of seminars for women. There were seminars to teach women

- How to dress for business

- How to handle money

- How to start a business

- How to climb the corporate ladder

- How to improve their office IQ

You name it—someone had planned a seminar around it!

I realized that slick marketers who had caught onto the fact that women were serious about their careers had found a new way to make money from it.

There were at least a dozen seminars offered each week for women in business. Among them, there were certainly a few good, informative courses. But it seemed to me that this new trend—seminars for business women—needed examination, if only to separate the wheat from the chaff. It would be a service to women, I felt, to attend the seminars, evaluate them, and report how effective they were. It would help women look more carefully at the ads and brochures before sending in their dollars. Also, I hoped, it would help them know what to expect for their money.

For three weeks, I attended seminars night and day, listening to the audience reactions as well as the performers. After careful analysis and many interviews, I was able to produce the story in Exhibit 17-2. By that time, fortunately, I was also able to prepare an objective rating chart of all the seminars I had attended. I believe it helped women in business make more responsible judgments, as the invitations to seminars continued to pour into their offices.

One of the best seminars I attended was presented by Mundelein College in Chicago, which has an excellent reputation for helping women return to the work force. Because of that record, it would have been a fine story for the college's public relations people to suggest—knowing that they would be rated well.

Most feature editors like to provide some informational service to their readers on a fairly regular basis. That's why you see lists of "weekend activities" on Fridays and lists of restaurants that serve special meals on Valentine's Day, Easter, Mother's Day, and Thanksgiving.

Similarly, depending on the audience, most publications also do seasonal lists. Magazines directed at parents might do a feature with a list of summer camps in spring or list "100 things to do with your kids" when school lets out in June.

Usually, such stories have a spritely lead of three or four paragraphs, to let the reader know what service the writer is going to provide—and why it's necessary. It's also useful, sometimes, to separate the story into several short stories, using separate headlines and separate graphics for each. That makes it easier for the reader to clip out and save the parts that interest him.

Among service stories I have found to work well are: an annual "things to do as a family," where to pick up a carry-out gourmet dinner in the city and surrounding suburbs, how to plant

EXHIBIT 17-1. Trend Story: Men Who Sew.

So much for macho, say sewing businessmen

By Sandra Pesmen

We're about to snitch that Chicago businessmen stitch.

Some hem and haw when you ask if they sew. But after a few mild denials and rationalizations, most draw themselves up, look you in the eye and blurt out, "Well, the finest tailors are men, aren't they?"

Yes, you agree, but those tailors at Hart Schaffner & Marx don't usually make circle cloths for the new table in the living room, decorator pillows, curtains for the kids' rooms, men's loungewear, or dresses for their daughters to wear to weddings.

"Well, they should!" exploded Lawrence Gold, a 48-year-old athletic insurance broker who works in Chicago and lives on the North Shore. "When the interior decorator came to our house and said he'd charge $70 for labor to make a cloth on our small round table, I told my wife he was nuts.

"I went to the store, looked at some cloths, bought some fabric and made the dumb thing in 20 minutes—for $10."

His wife Nancy didn't like the idea. It made her uncomfortable to watch her husband sew since she, a former model, can't. "But I explained it's a craft, like making model airplanes, and running the machine is mechanical," he said. "Now I fix all the seams our kids split in their clothes and I sew buttons on too. I was a bachelor a long time before I got married."

His neighbor, a 37-year-old attorney who handles estates for several prominent sports figures, has made tablecloths, curtains, decorator pillows, men's loungewear and even a party dress for his seven-year-old. More skittish than Mr. Gold, he asked that his name not be used.

"My grandfathers were tailors, my father was a furrier and my mother was a designer," he said. "There were always a lot of sewing machines around. I had to take sewing in home economics in eighth grade and I was good at it, but I didn't sew again until 1976 when our kids needed Halloween costumes. I made them, and they were so good the PTA asked me to design costumes for its annual play. After that I started sewing whenever we needed something because it's cheaper and we get original design and better quality."

He admitted he made the party dress in desperation. "We had no trouble finding suits for the boys to wear to a family wedding, but when we started trying to buy a little girl's dress we were shocked at how expensive and poorly made they were. So I made an evening pajama outfit for her, of matte jersey with an organdy overblouse, for about $13."

These men are not alone, although there are no solid statistics available yet. Spokesmen for Singer Co., Stretch and Sew Fabric Centers, and McCall's Pattern Co. report they see more businessmen sewing. More and more men are buying both machines and patterns for themselves—and taking sewing lessons at local sewing centers.

All the spokesmen said that although inflation has been a great incentive, most of the "male sewers" are enjoying it as a hobby too.

Justin Lear, Singer's regional operations manager for the North Central United States, observed that in the past three or four years there's been an upswing in men taking Singer's sewing classes. "Four years ago there were none. Now we see two or three popping up in a class of 20," he estimated.

Cindy Offolter, manager of the Oak Park Singer Sewing Center, said she sees more men coming in with their wives for the free lessons. "But recently I had two men come in to purchase machines for themselves," she said.

One, 34-year-old Bob Miller, a psychologist and program administrator for Mile Square Health Center Inc. at 2045 W. Washington, bought a $450 "economy version of the top line" from Ms. Offolter, then signed up for and completed the entire six-session, $39.95 course on how to sew.

"I'm not self conscious about sewing," Mr. Miller emphasized. "I started out mending sails for my boat. Then I made camping clothes and equipment. Now I make jogging suits, shirts, anything. I like clothes and go to fashion shows, and since the price of clothes has skyrocketed, I started to sew more."

It helps that Mr. Miller is a "macho man."

"People see me as a fairly macho character, so I'm free to do a variety of things. I'm comfortable with myself and I don't have any trouble with sewing as a sexual issue," he said. "I'm a mechanic, I can fix anything that can get broken, so I guess I have dexterity with sewing.

"I think the trend of men sewing is an offshoot of the women's rights movement. The message is clearly that as women attain greater freedom and rights that frees men up to do other things too. That's where I see it."

Ms. Offolter's other male student, 37-year-old Lewis Madison of Oak Park, didn't take more than two free lessons. "I sew my own way," said the "hobby tailor" who works at Audy Home. "I bought the machine for myself two months ago because we have four growing children and it was a need. My wife does hand needlework, but she doesn't make clothes." Mr. Madison paid $600 for the top of the line, and estimates that in five months he will have saved that amount in the family's clothes bills. "I made a dress for our daughter to wear to the prom in June," he said.

Carol Johnson, sewing instructor at Singer's Woodfield store, said a northwest suburban furniture salesman, who asked to remain anonymous, was her prize pupil. "He's completed four sets of classes, which

EXHIBIT 17-1 (Continued)

lasted 18 continuous weeks, but stopped for the summer," she said. "He always made draperies, bedspreads and now that he's learned the basics of sewing he makes everything for the family. It's a lovely hobby and he's enjoying it ."

Some men are clumsy with their fingers until they begin to realize that construction from a pattern is similar to that of model airplanes, she pointed out. And sometimes they are too embarrassed to concentrate.

"I had one student who was 6 foot 10, and he came for lessons because it's so expensive to buy extra long clothes," she remembered. "He had trouble fitting under the cabinet and we kept tripping over his feet. But the real problem was his wife came with him and I think she was embarrassed about having him in the class as the only man. He quit, but if he'd have come alone he'd have been all right."

Alice Straka, manager of Stretch and Sew Fabric Center in Lincolnwood, added that although her store is in an affluent suburb, people there have been dismayed by the jump in the price of ready-to-wear clothing and are trying to combat it by sewing.

"We have a lot of husbands and wives coming in together," she reports. "One man got so mad at his wife for not letting him use the family machine, he bought his own machine. Then he started buying more fabric than she did."

Ms. Straka insists nobody teases the men in her classes. In fact they're barely noticed now. "Four years go we had very few patterns for men, and few of them sewing. But now we carry a full wardrobe line including pants with pleats, vests, jackets, shirts—everything. And men especially seem to like the quick, easy way Stretch and Sew patterns fit together without all the old details."

Source: *Crain's Chicago Business,* Aug. 6, 1979, pp. 21–22.

EXHIBIT 17-2. Trend Story: Women Who Know.

Coaches fumble their get-ahead seminars

By Sandra Pesmen

The leaders of the seemingly endless women's seminars, conferences and workshops sprouting up all over the Chicago area are like coaches of a losing football team.

They know you need talent to win and they know there are only a few good players available. But they think if they pep everyone up with cheers and teach them the right plays—they'll win.

Like coaches, some of them once played on a winning team. Others teach because they didn't. Some do it because it's a way to earn money, others like the ego trip. A few are dedicated.

But—like the fans at Soldier Field these days—those who pay to get in are the ones being ripped off most of the time.

The greatest problem—which few seem to have solved—is that no one seems to know what leagues they're playing in. Many seminars geared for the minor leagues attract pros. A lot of heavies fall for slick sales promotion brochures and then are bored in the bush leagues.

Seminars should be geared to women in different career levels. Some should help women in entry levels, others should be aimed at middle management, a few should help the small minority of women in upper management.

Few seminars fill the need. Most are a hodge-podge of lectures and slide films featuring cheerleader types dressed in suits, waving pointers and shouting cliches. They talk in generalities on nebulous subjects such as "Awareness in a Woman's World," "Women and Change," "Images," "Investment Dressing," "Networking," "Keeping Your Sense of Humor in Business" and "An Ounce of Image Is Worth a Pound of Performance."

Much of this is insulting to management or professional women. Take the state's first day-long Women's Career Conference on a recent Saturday that attracted 250 working women.

Most who came and paid the $15 registration fee have secretarial jobs, earn between $10,000 and $18,000 and have children to support. The day was arranged by Sharon Sharp, special assistant to the governor on women.

To her credit, Ms. Sharp attracted several successful business leaders to volunteer their time to lead worthwhile morning workshops on employment opportunities, education and technical training necessary to gain jobs.

But Ms. Sharp also chose Michigan Avenue's high-priced hairdresser Paul Glick (who happens to be her own personal "image consultant") to deliver the keynote address on "An Ounce of Image is Worth a Pound of Performance."

EXHIBIT 17-2 (Continued)

Mr. Glick's presentation included a simultaneous two-slide film production showing successful women who wear the right clothes and makeup and unsuccessful eomen who don't. Mr. Glick closed with the suggestion that the women in the audience begin planning their fall wardrobe by writing $1,000 on a piece of paper. Then he told them to list one blazer, two pair of slacks, one blouse and one silk dress. When the audience seemed bewildered, he said, "What's the matter? Wouldn't you invest $1,000 in yourselves? If you won't you'll probably stay in lower positions. You're not concerned enough about your presentation."

Judy Markowitz, a small slim woman with short curly hair wearing green slacks and a print blouse, stood up and protested, "I realize I may be in the minority here but some of the things you said are very offensive to me. You stress packaging women using stereotypes created by those in power who are men. We want to advance substance in careers, not beauty stereotypes."

Women also were upset at the seminar for "Career Women in the Modern Business World" which was held later that week called "Awareness in a Woman's World" sponsored by the Sales and Marketing Executives of Chicago (SME).

The day was suggested and beautifully choreographed by SME member Sandy Karn, who is director of Creative Results Sources Inc. It drew more than 300 working women from five states.

Let's skip over the fact that Ms. Karn's visibility and positive performance aren't going to hurt her own business. The lady still gets points for demanding that SME sponsor the day because it sponsors similar days for men. And she gets a gold star for bringing out Barbara Proctor, founder, creative director and president of Proctor & Gardner Advertising Inc.

Ms. Karn gave the women profile tests to help them understand their ability to dominate and influence others and to perform tasks with steadiness and compliance. It is an effective tool Ms. Karn also uses in talks before businessmen.

Ms. Proctor explained that if women are to succeed in business, most must begin self-improvement with re-evaluation. She suggested discarding or limiting personal relationships that interfere with a career, and increasing relationships that will accelerate career goals. She outlined realistic risks involved in goal setting and emphasized that as one gains personal skills and confidence, the risks diminish.

But Ms. Karn has to take some demerits for fleshing out the $40, day-long program with brain-washing, time-wasting entertainers who travel the professional speakers circuit at the going rate of $750 plus travel and hotel expenses.

Patricia Fripp, an English-born San Francisco barber and beauty shop owner, once voted one of San Francisco's 10 sexiest ladies, opened the day with a talk called "Take Charge of Your Life," laced with anecdotes, jokes and encouragement that brinked on a song and dance routine.

Later Jeanne Robertson of North Carolina, billed as "a former Miss America loser who was named Miss Congeniality and is 6 feet 2 inches tall," entertained. Her stand-up humiliation routine made fun of her height, her former participation in beauty contests and her role as foolish wife.

"I was humiliated for her when she stood there making fun of herself," said a real estate saleswoman. "I wanted to cry. And I found my palms were sweating. I didn't find anything funny about it."

But there are some worthwhile seminars available to women, and not all are expensive. Many are presented by universities and colleges and fit conveniently into women's work schedules.

One such was Learning at Lunchtime, a noontime mini-series in management recently held at Roosevelt University. Part of the university's non-credit programs, the five-session series focused on assertiveness, coping with stress, management skills, coping with harassment and strategies for promotion. Taught by Marie Kisiel, a Roosevelt University professor, it cost $25 per seminar and attendees were invited to bring a bag lunch.

The 24 women attending the first session were in supervisory and mid-management positions. They were given specific examples of ways to determine if they have the skills and personality traits necessary for management roles. Ms. Kisiel also outlined ways in which women may attain and further develop those skills.

Similar conferences are sponsored regularly at Mundelein College and Northwestern University's Division of Continuing Education.

Ruth Ratny, 1979 Advertising Woman of the Year who owns two successful businesses, has made a third business out of women-only seminars on "Everything You Have to Know to Own Your Own Business."

Although Ms. Ratny admits frankly that her first interest is money, she gives her customers their money's worth. In addition to sound professional advice from her own experience and that of other businesswomen who have "made it," she provides outlines giving complete information on banking, financing, legal requirements, purchasing and marketing procedures.

Outspoken Elaine Berger, director of special programs for Mundelein College, despairs over the plethora of poor seminars for women. "Oh my, there's a lot of junk around," she moaned. "A few years ago it was conferences to help blacks—now it's women."

Ms. Berger believes there's too much emphasis on dressing up and learning buzzwords.

Source: *Crain's Chicago Business,* Nov. 12, 1979, pp. 23–24.

EXHIBIT 17-2 (Continued)

"What offends me is that the women who come to these things get hurt," Ms. Berger said. "They really want better jobs. They need better jobs and need self-confidence. But in no way do most of these seminars address themselves to the kinds of issues that will give women that help."

This educator asks consumers to be wary of people who have a money-making interest in giving seminars. She suggests checking the credentials of everyone on each panel before sending in your registration check. (And remember that even though the literature usually stresses the fee is tax deductible, it's still out-of-pocket money for people who have little ability to take advantage of this tax break.)

If the seminar's goals are not clear, call or write ahead of time to make sure it is offering information that will serve some need in your own career plan.

"Consider yourselves consumers," Ms. Berger said. "Investigate. Try it on. Take a good look. Kick the tires. If you buy an appliance you go to *Consumer Reports*. If you want career counseling, go to a respected college and talk with professional counselors. And make sure it's an institution that has credibility in terms of doing things for women."

Local seminars for women

SEMINAR	COST	GEARED TO	RUN BY	RATING
Learning at Lunchtime: A Mini-Series in Management	$25 per session	Women who hope to improve management skills.	Roosevelt University Non-Credit Division	Sincere effort aimed at a specific group; delivers the helpful information promised.
Women-Only Seminar on Business Ownership	$85	Women who have acquired special skills and are ready to begin their own businesses.	Ruth L Ratny	Although the seminars do provide important information delivered by professionals, much of it can be acquired from texts.
State of Illinois Women's Career Conference	$15	Every woman in the state who has worked, is working, or plans to.	Governor's Office of Interagency Cooperation	Failed in its efforts to be all things to all working women. The morning sessions were helpful.
Prime Time	$10	Several workshops, each geared to a specific audience, led by a professional who volunteered the time.	Mundelein College	Attracted more than 450 women who were so satisfied most will return for other seminars. Time carefully devoted to each level of careers.
Awareness in a Woman's World	$40	Supervisors and middle management, small-business owners.	Sales and Marketing Executives of Chicago	Talks by Chicago businesswomen educational and inspirational. Entertainment talks a waste of time.
W.O.M.A.N., Woman, Owner, Manager, Administrator, Networking	$1.50	All working women.	Three Chicago working women attempting to set up a "network"	Well-intentioned, but misses the mark as a real help to the advanced or semi-professional on her way up. There was a lot of fantasizing about the simplicity of beginning a business.
Today's Agenda Shop's Mini-Seminars	Free	Women who work.	I. Magnin	Talks on images, "investment dressing," fitness survival and makeup geared to bringing the working women into the store dwell more on cliches than information.
Women and Change	$36	Women who want to bring about advancement through learning exchanges.	Seminars R You Enterprises	Oops. Not enough people responded to the answering service and P.O. Box, so it was called off two days before.

This chart is designed to give readers a sense of the wide variety of seminars and meetings offered to Chicago working women. For three weeks *Crain's Chicago Business* monitored meetings, listened to speakers and talked with attendees to evaluate the programs. The ratings are a result of those interviews.

a garden of gourmet vegetables suitable for your Cuisinart suppers, and how to find dependable household and personal services—"Where to Find a Wife."

Always remember which publications do service features, make sure your clients are included when the service is appropriate, and try to write your own service features.

An example of a *Crain's Chicago Business* service feature, on preparing a gourmet ethnic picnic, is shown in Exhibit 17-3. I interviewed five of Chicago's leading ethnic chefs, asked what they would take on a picnic in their native lands, and then printed their comments and favorite recipes.

Essay features impart interesting and useful information but usually do so with some personal touches and include some definite impressions of the author.

In some cases, the feature writer "stacks" the deck with information that supports his view—but he makes that clear at the beginning of the story.

The essay can include a variety of forms, even some that haven't been invented yet. Essays may be written in the first or third person. Sometimes, to increase tension, the italicized thoughts of the writer are inserted throughout the story in counterpoint to the hard facts of the situation.

In any event, the essay feature is "a good read" that usually leaves the reader thinking some pro and con thoughts about the subject. In addition, many feature writers consider it the most creative and satisfying kind of journalism a reporter can write.

An example of an essay feature dealing with a serious problem of particular relevance to people in the business community is shown in Exhibit 17-4.

Obviously, some personal feelings about John Fischetti colored the lead in this story. But notice also the following themes:

- Why some people take a long time getting over the death of a colleague

- How such a tragedy resembles a death in the family

- What some corporations did when death struck their offices

- What executives should look for among employees when a death occurs and how they can help them

Once again, a poignant quote was saved to add impact as a snapper finish.

EXHIBIT 17-3. Service Feature: A Gourmet Picnic.

Pack up your basket with an ethnic picnic mix

Frankly, picnic baskets stuffed with hot dogs, peanut butter sandwiches, potato chips and marshmallows have gotten a bit tiring.

So *Crain's Chicago Business* Features Editor Sandra Pesmen asked three of Chicago's finest ethnic chefs to prepare more inspired fare with their favorite native foods.

And they responded with enthusiasm in three dialects:

"Ahhh, zis eez an exciting concept," said Lucien Verge, French owner of L'Escargot in the Allerton Hotel. "I luff to pack you a Hungarian basket," beamed flamboyant Chef Louis Szathmary, owner of The Bakery, 2118 N. Lincoln Ave. . . . "No problem," was the answer of George Kuan, who with partner Austin Koo recently opened the Chinese Hunan Palace at 1050 N. State.

Bon appetit!

Try Drunken Chicken from the Orient

Authentic Chinese meals include so many courses—each with such a wide variety of foods—that a wise diner never eats more than one or two bites of any dish.

And the picnic prepared by George Kuan, who with his partner Austin Koo owns three House of Hunan restaurants and the Hunan Palace in Newberry Plaza, was no exception.

George got busy on his extensive menu as soon as he had packed Tsing-Tao Beer from the Mainland, Taiwan Beer from the island, and a few bottles of delicious fruity Tai-Shan white wine from the top of the tallest mountain in Hopeh Province north of the Yangtze River.

This elaborate Chinese meal began with assorted cold salads placed on a black lacquered wooden Lazy

EXHIBIT 17-3 (Continued)

Susan. These included finely sliced chicken and crisp cucumbers, dainty jellyfish and chicken with bits of bright orange carrots, ham with bean sprouts and a delicate salad made of transparent green pea noodles in sesame sauce.

After these had been placed on a bamboo place mat, along wih side dishes containing hot red pepper, dark soy, yellow sesame mustard and sweet-sour sauces, George shook out some red linen napkins with a flourish—and introduced his second course.

This was a tray of foods that had been well marinated in hot, tangy Five Spice Sauce. This sauce is made from George's own recipe and remains in the refrigerator for several weeks as a marinade for many foods.

Included were beef and tongue, sliced thin and served cold (which tasted much like kosher pastrami), reddish brown chicken wings and legs and boiled eggs that had turned the dark brown color of the marinade on the outside, but retained a bright white color on the inside and offered a pungent soy flavor.

The main course at this picnic was "Drunken Chicken" made from a fresh, full-breasted capon. "We call it 'Drunken Chicken' because it's soaked in wine sauce overnight," George explained.

It was hard to keep a straight face when this talented chef invited us to taste his picnic with the usual Chinese greeting, "Please excuse us for our humble offering—and forgive us our terrible food."

He added, "It's traditional for Chinese chefs to deprecate themselves. It would be considered bad manners for a Chinese to brag about his cooking as Americans do."

Drunken Chicken

    1 large 3–5 lb. chicken or capon (freshly killed)
    6–8 cups clear chicken stock
    1½ cups cold chicken broth
    1½ cups rice wine (Shaohsing brand) or dry sherry
    2–3 tbsp. salt (to taste)

Preparation: Wash and dry the chicken. Place a metal spoon in the chicken's cavity to help retain heat while cooking.

Bring chicken stock to boil, using a stewing pot that is large enough to cover the entire chicken with stock.Submerge chicken, breast-side down in boiling stock. Cover pot and bring liquid to boil again. Allow to boil for 2–3 minutes. Then lower heat and allow to simmer for 20 minutes. Leaving chicken in pot, allow to cool at least 2 hours.

Remove chicken from broth. Remove spoon. Cut chicken into eight pieces, discarding the back. Sprinkle salt (to taste) over entire chicken. Broth may be saved in a tightly sealed container in the refrigerator. Combine equal parts of wine and cold chicken broth, making enough marinade to cover the chicken.

Submerge chicken in marinade. Sprinkle additional teaspoon of salt on top. Cover tightly and refrigerate for a minimum of one day and as long as one month. When ready to eat, remove from marinade and cut into bite-size pieces. When serving, cover with spoonful of marinade and garnish with sprigs of fresh coriander. (Marinade may be saved for reuse. Just be sure to reboil for sterilization purposes and add more wine.)

Dipping sauces: Drunken chicken may be served with a selection of sauces, including Hunan chili sauce, available in Oriental food stores, and the Hunan Five Spice Sauce.

Bring a monkfish from L'Escargot

Lucien Verge, owner of L'Escargot, believes that "since picnics are light and joyous occasions, the food must be in the same vein."

The first item he placed in his basket was a corkscrew. The next items were a loaf of crusty French bread, fresh fruit and a small wooden board to hold Brie cheese.

Next he packed a bottle of Rose of Parovance from the south of France to drink with the meal—and a bottle of Lillet (a vermouth) and a bottle of Pastis to serve as aperitifs.

Lucien believes everyone attending a picnic should participate in its preparation, and he suggested that children who can't cook yet should go into the fields to gather wild flowers. Then he packed a small simple vase to display the flowers.

His picnic began with puff pastries filled with either anchovies or Swiss cheese and sweet red pimentos.

The first serious course was cold poached monkfish, the poor man's lobster, because "since cold lobster is delicious, cold monkfish is also."

The fish was placed on a platter with slices of juicy tomatoes and red onion, then sprinkled with black Mediterranean olives, fresh basil and light oil and vinegar dressing.

Next came a cup of cold beet borsht.

The main feature of Lucien's picnic was a tray of chicken breast and roast beef. The cold supreme chicken *chaud-froid* (breast of chicken poached in broth) was skinned, cleaned, glazed, then decorated with sweet red pimento and tarragon leaf. The cold, rare beef was sliced, then garnished with cucumber salad mayonnaise, aspic and hard-boiled eggs.

The Brie had a place of honor at the center of the table, because the French believe "cheese is like a guest in your house—you must treat it nicely."

And because "dessert is frivolous," Lucien brought a glass bowl filled with fresh raspberries and ripe peaches that had been marinated in Grenache wine, then sweetened with a touch of sugar and Metaxa, a Greek cognac.

EXHIBIT 17-3 (Continued)

Chicken Chaud-Froid

(serves four)

4 double, fresh, boned breasts of chicken
Enough water to cover chicken
1 stick celery
1 carrot
1 bay leaf
1 small sprig parsley
6 oz. white wine
Salt and pepper to taste
Sauce
2 tbsp. flour
½ pint whipping cream
3 tbsp. butter or 1 fresh sweet red pepper or small
   can of sweet red pepper
2 tbsp. gelatine

Chicken method: Put chicken in casserole with water, white wine, and all ingredients except sauce ingredients.

Simmer till chicken is cooked, 10 to 15 minutes. Cool in broth. Remove chicken and place on flat tray. Remove skin and trim. Press gently. Place a saucer with a small weight on each for about half an hour.

Sauce method: Melt butter, then add flour and cook 2 or 3 minutes, while stirring with wisk. Pour in 1½ cups strained hot chicken broth, bring to boil, simmer 10 minutes and stir in gelatin. Strain again and cool on ice. When cool but not cold, add whipping cream. Check seasoning, and add what's necessary. Set out chicken, spoon cold sauce over it once or twice and place in refrigerator. Repeat at least twice, until smooth, uniform glaze forms. Decorate with a few blanched leaves of tarragon, or sweet red pepper.

Outdoor Hungarian feast features pork, red pepper

Mention "picnic" to The Bakery owner Chef Louis Szathmary, and his eyes twinkle, his walrus mustache quivers and a big grin shoots across his merry face.

"We Hungarians make almost the whole picnic at one time on a spit. We call it the Outdoorsman's Grill," he explains. Then he describes the way his family used to go out into the woods, build a fire and lay "good thick dark bread" on the grill to toast. "At the same time we cut a V-shaped twig and prop the spit through it so the grease from the bacon on the skewer drops down on the toast while it's cooking."

Hungarians bring bottles of red wine along on a picnic—and mix it (half and half) with chilled Borsec Romanian natural sparkling mineral water to make spritzers for the grown-ups. "Children drink the sparkling water mixed with lemon and sugar," the chef says.

Chef Louis always packs a salad, made of more raw green peppers, sweet white knob onions and sliced tomatoes in a light vinegar dressing. He also includes some Hungarian mustard, made one day before the picnic. Hard-cooked eggs are also tucked into his basket, to be dipped in the mustard sauce, and he usually adds a strange and wonderful Hungarian cheese spread called *liptoi*, made of *feta* cheese, butter, mustard, paprika, onions and caraway seeds.

Outdoorsman's Grill

(serves 4)
12 oz. pork tenderloin
salt, pepper and paprika to taste
2 to 3 tbsp. corn oil
8 oz. smoked Hungarian sausage or Polish sausage
   or 4 smokey links
8 oz. of Hungarian or regular slab bacon, unsliced
   or smoked jaw
4 knob onions
1 red bell pepper cut into quarters
4 skewers at least 14 inches
8 slices European type bread

Method: Cut pork tenderloin into 12-inch medallions, gently pound them until they are 2½ inches in diameter.

Sprinkle lightly with salt, pepper and paprika on both sides. Brush with corn oil, place in small plastic container and pour rest of oil on top. Chill.

Cut sausage into 8 equal pieces.

Cut bacon into four pieces, leaving rind on. With rind down, cut ½-inch-deep gashes crosswise in both directions in bacon about ¼ inch apart. Do not cut through. With tip of sharp knife, make a small hole in the center of each piece of bacon through the rind.

Clean the onions and with pointed knife cut a hole through on diagonal to ease the skewer through the whole onion.

On the day of the picnic, divide all ingredients into four and put on each skewer three pork tenderloin medallions, two pieces of sausage, a quarter of red bell pepper and a knob onion, finishing the top with a piece of bacon.

Let coals burn down until all black spots completely disappear and a layer of gray ash covers the glowing red center of each coal. Hold the skewer over coals and keep turning. When fat starts to drip from bacon, hold it over a thick slice of previously toasted rye bread and let the drippings be absorbed by the bread.

Many people eat this first slice of bread with thick slices of raw tomatoes, cucumbers, green or ripe red peppers and sliced onions or knob onions as a "first course." When the meat on the skewer is done and the bacon turns crisp, eat the meat and vegetables.

Source: *Crain's Chicago Business*, July 20, 1981, pp. 25–28.

EXHIBIT 17-4. Essay Feature: Death in the Office.

A death in the office is like a loss in the family

By Sandra Pesmen

Every day at noon, after finishing preliminary work on his daily sketch, Pulitzer Prize-winning political cartoonist John Fischetti sauntered over to a front booth in Riccardo's bar and held court over lunch with the likes of Mike Royko and Bill Mauldin.

Other journalists hovered at the sides of the booth, catching waves and smiles from John, delighted to hear bits of his witty stories and raucous reminiscences.

And on the way back to his drawing board at the Chicago *Sun-Times*, John seemed never too busy to stop and listen to his colleagues' ideas for cartoons.

It was no wonder, then, that when John Fischetti died of a heart attack on Nov. 18, 1980, those who knew him felt a personal loss.

They knew the 64-year-old John had a heart condition—but still, they gathered in shocked sorrow about the coffee machines, unable to believe the news.

Standard office protocol followed. Obituaries were printed and notices went up on bulletin boards announcing memorial services at Fourth Presbyterian Church.

When the final tributes were over, that was supposed to be it. Everyone was expected to go back to work and forget their loss.

So why did John Fischetti's close associates find themselves looking sadly at the room that had been his office long after it was redecorated? Why do some of them still have trouble sitting in "his booth" in Riccardo's?

Death doesn't go away simply because the service is over and the boss says it's time to get back to work. Death in the office inspires as much prolonged sorrow as a death in the family.

In fact, recovery from this kind of extended depression often requires the same overt grieving—"thinking and talking through"—as does the death of a relative.

"Emotions in the office will vary, depending upon the deceased's age, responsibilities and personal relationships," says Dr. George Pollock, who has studied the problem at the Chicago Institute for Psychoanalysis.

"And if the one who dies is still comparatively young and productive—cut down before his promise is fulfilled—then there can be feelings of anger at fate, and disappointment, as well as sorrow that must be worked through.

"Also, if the deceased was a strong, respected person in a high-ranking job, his absence may affect everyone in the office. In addition to feeling that they have lost a friend, some employees may feel frightened, as if they've also lost the firm's guiding parent-figure."

Many people felt exactly that way at the Dec. 29 death of Frank Aldrich, 56-year-old internationally known chief executive of Kemper Reinsurance Co. in Long Grove, a subsidiary of Kemper Corp.

"You have to understand that, while there are 2,500 people at Kemper, there are only about 100 in our department, and we've been pretty much isolated from the primary companies," says a bereaved colleague of Mr. Aldrich. "We in this company have been a family, and he was the head of it from the beginning."

When word of Mr. Aldrich's death reached the office at 8:30 in the morning, there was a stunned silence, then people began to weep; some literally reached out to one another to counter their sense of loss. "I saw a lot of touching, hugging and simple kindness," says the colleague.

While the Kemper people struggled with their emotions, the news spread. They had to deal with telephoned condolences and telex messages from all over the world.

But there also was a welcome sense of continuity and stability, because December is the busiest season of the year for reinsurance companies—and work had to go on.

In fact, most people in the Kemper "family" struggled through their sorrow, trying to work harder and better than ever before because, says a spokesman, "Frank would have wanted it that way. There was a sense of 'doing it for the Gipper.'"

In this case, there were few fears of what would happen with a new chief executive, because Mr. Aldrich had long been grooming 43-year-old Dave Mathis as his successor. But while the general leadership remained intact, a few employees faced more difficult transitions.

That was the case for Mary Stough, Mr. Aldrich's personal secretary for 20 years.

"I had planned to take early retirement in March, although I hadn't told anyone yet, and might have changed my mind if this hadn't happened," she says. "But when Mr. Aldrich

EXHIBIT 17-4 (Continued)

died, I announced my retirement immediately, and didn't even have to consider it. The new man brought his own secretary."

Similar feelings of sorrow mixed with anxiety struck Ann Scanlon, a legal secretary at Lord Bissell & Brook, after her boss, 49-year-old attorney Les Zaczek, died of a heart attack while at lunch last October.

"I'd been in Europe on vacation, and I came home the evening of the day of the funeral so I didn't get to see him. That made it difficult for me, because I kept looking up, expecting to see him come in. Even now, I sometimes have the feeling he'll be coming into the office, and I still miss him. I had worked as his secretary four years, we'd been working on projects together since 1954."

Mr. Zaczek's untimely death created a particular crisis for Ms. Scanlon because she didn't know for whom she'd be working. "I knew I'd always have a job at this firm, but I wondered who my new boss would be and whether we'd get along as well as Les and I had.

"The policy here was to let me wait until there was another opening as a private secretary, and I did that. Everyone was most kind and no one pressured me, and I began to work for another man Jan. 1."

Ms. Scanlon, who expects to work at the firm at least 10 more years before retiring, still feels a deep sense of loss. "Les was like an extension of my own family. I spent the better part of every weekday working with him. You don't get over that immediately."

Sometimes when a colleague dies, contemporaries, particularly those past 40, begin to feel their own mortality. "That's because they're in the front lines now, and this situation certainly underlines that," says Dr. Pollock.

That's why they gather around the coffee machine and murmur, "He smoked three packs a day," "He didn't exercise" and "He was always overeating." It's as if they're telling themselves that if they stop smoking, eat properly and start to exercise, they won't die.

Sometimes, colleagues of the deceased are moved to re-examine their lifestyles, values and career goals. They consider whether they are using their time correctly.

That's what Mark Satterthwaite did. Mr. Satterthwaite became chairman of the department of managerial economics and decision sciences at Northwestern University's J. L. Kellogg Graduate School of Management after the death Dec. 7, 1981, of 42-year-old Chairwoman Nancy L. Schwartz.

"I had worked closely with Nancy almost 10 years. She was one of the architects of this department, with an international reputation. We were so shocked by her sudden, untimely death that everyone talked about it and felt grieved about it for a long time.

"But it also made all of us in the department ask ourselves why we're doing what we are doing when we may die tomorrow. I'm 36, and it made me take another look at the reality of death and the quality of my life. A lot of us did. I began to examine how my life was balanced between personal and professional time and to wonder what kinds of limits I want to place on professional commitments."

While much has been done to make people aware that when a loved one dies, grief and sorrow must be worked through by communication and conscious grieving, not many companies realize that their employees often require a similar catharsis when death strikes the office.

"We have no formal programs to help people when a fellow employee dies, but we are aware of the impact that it carries," says Dr. Fern Asma, assistant health director of Illinois Bell Telephone Co. "When that happens, everyone is given time off to attend the funeral and management tries to be very supportive. Managers are expected to go over and talk with employees who seem disturbed afterward. If they notice anyone is particularly affected, they alert us and we intervene."

Certainly it helps fellow workers when a company sends notices of a death throughout the office, gives people time off to attend a funeral and prepares a memorial service. The Kellogg School even has established a memorial fund for Professor Schwartz.

But too many firms still betray a myopic view of the subject.

Observes one secretary in a prestigious Chicago accounting firm: "They always send a notice around to everyone when a partner dies—but last year, when a secretary died of cancer, there wasn't a word mentioned anywhere."

Source: *Crain's Chicago Business*, Feb. 8, 1982, pp. 26–27.

EXERCISE 17-1

List three new trends you've noticed.

Among some of the trends I've seen that can be turned into feature stories are:

- More weddings among young people, fewer live-togethers

- More young couples giving up the two-person income and having a baby—*and* arranging for the mother to stay home to care for it

- More empty nesters moving to the city for Monday-to-Friday work and activities—but keeping their home in the suburbs for weekend living

- Burglaries increasing generally, particularly during holiday times, when Northerners make holiday trips to the sunbelt. There are some new trends developing as people who are burglarized decide to protect themselves.

Choose one trend and write a feature story about it. Interview the authorities in the field and some people who have been personally affected by the trend. Include some anecdotes.

Write your story in 600 to 750 words.

EXERCISE 17-2

Everyone has some special interest; so choose one of your own and write a service piece about it.

It may be on opera, theater, art, sailing, running, or hockey.

Plan your service story and "how to" listing around that subject.

Interview authorities in the field, as well as participants in it. Talk to some people who don't like it at all, in order to get both pros and cons for your story. Next, think about what you like best about the subject and try to get that across to your reader. Also consider how you can point out negative aspects of the subject—and tell the reader to avoid them.

Begin with a lead that attracts the reader and, at the same time, informs him about what you're going to do. Then feed information in a simple way, including a list of the options and costs to the participant.

A good length for such a piece is about 750 words. A sidebar list should include at least five contacts.

EXERCISE 17-3

The most difficult part about creating an essay feature is finding a suitable subject that you have some real feelings about and will interest the readers.

Think about the things that are on your mind and on the minds of other people you come in contact with. For example:

- Is your neighborhood changing in some way?

- Is there anything about your career that's disturbing you?

- Have you noticed a medical or emotional problem that's becoming a trend?

- Is there some new activity your colleagues have started participating in, such as a new sport or hobby?

- Is there someone representative of an interesting group that you may interview?

Using all of the lessons you've learned so far, write a story based on one of the suggested topics in 750 words. If you have really developed into a feature writer/reporter by now, your biggest problem will be keeping it short.

Chapter 18

Breaking the Rules

Sometimes, in an effort to surprise and please readers, feature editors try to do something wildly different. We call them "off-the-wall" stories, and bright publicists can certainly suggest them to us regularly. Many do.

One popular "off-the-wall" feature at *Crain's Chicago Business* is the annual Christmas Trivia Quiz, which can be geared to any audience. It contains questions about the Chicago business community and includes tests about people, places, things, and events in that category. The prize is dinner for four at one of the city's best restaurants. The quiz meets with great enthusiasm.

Another "off-the-wall" feature was "The Great City-Suburban House Swap." It was based on my husband's and my experience of moving into a small, old house in Chicago's Old Town for a week, while the owners of that house moved into our modern suburban home.

Sometimes, we gather a group of people with one common denominator for an "off-the-wall" story. Such was the case for the piece about "unsung heroes" in Exhibit 18-1. Each "hero" was a person who made the day brighter for Chicago business people simply by trying to be pleasant. (A good publicist could find several such people in his clients' firms and have them ready when he makes the suggestion.)

We used the same method to create a tribute to business people who had retired and yet continued to live very productive lives and serve as examples to everyone who will eventually face retirement (see Exhibit 18-2).

Reading most of the feature story examples given so far, you can see a pattern emerging that shows: a lead, some transitional paragraphs introducing and explaining the subject, some colorful dialogue, and some anecdotes to lead the reader into the essence of the subject.

But remember that there are exceptions to all rules. And if you have the spectacular talent necessary to make the subject come alive through a very different approach—that is always respected and admired.

A good example is the business feature story by Steve Yahn, former Crain Communications publisher, and now editor of the *Pittsburgh Business Times*, who wrote the story when he was a reporter for the *Chicago Daily News*.

The story has no specific lead, with a neat five-W summary for the reader. I don't believe Yahn sat down and outlined his themes, and I'm pretty sure he didn't think too carefully about how he was going to develop tension and build bits of the story to a climax. Nor did he consciously plan a snapper finish. In this case, genius played its part. The poetic effort flowed from the wordsmith's typewriter, creating a piece that ran in the financial pages but would have been at home anywhere in most newspapers or magazines.

EXHIBIT 18-1. "Off-the-Wall" Story: Unsung Heroes.

CCB salutes Chicago's troop of unsung heroes

By Sandra Pesmen

Some days nothing goes right. The basement floods, the stock market falls, the RTA raises fares and the Kennedy Expressway backs up.

Just when you think you can't stand another moment—an unsung hero smiles, says something kind and goes out of the way to create a pleasant moment in your business day.

He or she may be the friendly busperson in a very ordinary cafeteria, the perky woman behind a coffee carryout counter, the conscientious deckhand on the Wendella commuter boat, a caring ad agency media buyer or a concerned company nurse.

No matter what their jobs, these people share a selfless desire to make "rainbows" in your day. And they do that when it's not actually part of their job and they're not required or expected to do it.

CRAIN'S CHICAGO BUSINESS salutes a small sampling of such unsung heroes here.

* * *

Faber's cafeteria in Union Station was not famous for its ambiance or special attention from its employees until Wladyslaw Lemek appeared early this year.

With a smile on his lips, and a pot of steaming coffee in his hands, he helped his "guests" to their places each day with a friendly "gooda murning."

Mr. Lemek, soon nicknamed "Walter" by his customers, came to Chicago from his home in Tarnow, Poland, because there were no jobs in his native land. And he was so happy to be working here, he shared his joy with those around him.

He was the first employee in the shop to hold chairs out for customers, to constantly wipe and shine the many tables and to refill coffee cups without being asked.

Walter also offered nods and smiles even though he had some difficulty understanding the new language surrounding him.

Although Walter and his regular customers exchanged few words, they eventually began to understand each other very well.

When he returned to Poland last month, he carried with him several gifts and cards from customers who had learned to depend upon his cheery daily greetings.

* * *

Ann Lachat is a company nurse who specializes in healing hurt feelings.

The 42-year-old medic stationed at CBS national studios, 630 McClurg Court, is revered by coworkers because she spends almost as much time attending to emotional wounds as she does to physical ones.

"Ann will listen to your problems when you drop in for an aspirin or a Band-Aid" said one CBS employee. "She's such a sympathetic person, and such a good listener. If you do go to her with a physical problem, she always gives you a book to read about it so you won't be frightened. And if she's talked with you about something, she'll always come by your office a few days later to see how you're feeling."

* * *

Twenty-eight-year-old Marilyn Palmer probably has as much reason as you do to grump and growl in the morning. The Waller High School grad last year completed her studies as a certified nurse's assistant, but she still hasn't found a job in that field of work.

But unless you ask, she never discusses her disappointment.

The perky, ever-smiling assistant manager of Boudin Bakery, 63 E. Chicago Ave., cheerfully cuts free samples of crusty sourdough bread each morning. Then she gives all customers a smile as she pours their coffee.

When a customer empties her purse to pay for the coffee, Marilyn quickly says, "It's empty now, but remember, pretty soon now, it's going to be filled up again."

* * *

EXHIBIT 18-1 (Continued)

When you come into Chicago at the O'Hare International Airport Terminal 1 and start going through customs, it's reassuring to see Patrolman Daniel F. Healy, his Irish face aglow, greeting the people in the lines, giving everyone a helping hand, assisting the elderly with their luggage and calling porters for those who need them.

"He's been there so many years, and he does much more than he has to to make you feel good, especially when you come in late at night," observes W. Clement Stone, the master of Positive Mental Attitude, who nominated Patrolman Healy as an unsung hero.

"He's a perfect example of what we call 'going that extra mile, giving that extra special effort.' "

*   *   *

If you need a lift any time during the business day, stop at the tobacco shop run by Eastern Newsstands in the lower level of the John Hancock Building, 875 N. Michigan, and watch Marion June Fox in action.

The 58-year-old saleswoman talks to all who venture near her counter. "Hi, Dolly," she says to the women, "Hi, Baby," she says to the men.

She knows her customers and their tastes so well that when they walk in she reaches down and gets their cigarettes without waiting for them to name the brand.

"Whenever I feel down in the dumps, I walk in there for the morning paper and by the time I leave, Marion's made me feel good," says one customer.

*   *   *

The people who work with Carol Oldberg at Zechman and Associates advertising agency call her their own Lone Ranger.

"She's constantly brightening everyone's life, in small but important ways, and she never lets anyone know about it," says her boss, Jan Zeckman. "After Carol quietly places a box of cookies on your desk, or brings in a cheesecake she baked for your birthday, she disappears. We're always saying, 'Where did that curly-haired girl come from, where did she go?' "

Most of the time, the 32-year-old media buyer is running on to do something nice for someone else.

Coworkers, customers and even people she buys space from receive constant small tokens of friendship from Ms. Oldberg.

One associate calls her "an all-around happy person, who brings small rainbows into the lives of people around her."

*   *   *

John Mack, 61, is a lesson in "Good fellow-Ship." The sweet-tempered deckhand on Wendella's commuter boat on the Chicago River between the Wrigley Building and the North Western Station, Mr. Mack goes out of his way to make every passenger feel special.

Riding the Sunliner since 1967, Mr. Mack has developed an unusual style, giving instant travelogues to anyone new to the river. "I know all the buildings and like to tell people what they are," he says.

Wearing his white cap and navy shirt, Mr. Mack takes special care of women and children.

While some others simply take tickets and silently unhook the ropes, John Mack stops to say a pleasant "Good morning" to each passenger. He often advises that they "have a nice day" and always holds the women's hands as they cross the plank on and off the docks.

Notes one rider, "That's really nice of him, since some of those others show so little concern you could fall right in."

Source: *Crain's Chicago Business,* Aug. 10, 1981, p. 39.

EXHIBIT 18-2. "Off-the-Wall" Story: Active Retirees.

Businessmen find the good life after first career ends

Whether we want to face it or not, aging is a disease we're all going to catch some day, and with it comes the issue of retirement.

For many, retirement is a time of fear, with a lifelong daily pattern disrupted.

To others it's a time of joy, offering an opportunity to do all those things that one just hasn't found the time for. . . .

In order to investigate some possibilities of retirement, CRAIN'S CHICAGO BUSINESS interviewed three business people. One founded a new company that takes more time—and gives him more monetary rewards—than his original career at Illinois Bell did. The second works as supervisor in a sheltered workshop, and the third spends much of his time at a very busy, productive senior center.

Ironically, now that they are at a stage where they can do anything that pleases them, all three men derive their greatest satisfaction from serving others.

Traveling on to a second career

By John Barron

A tall, lean, well-dressed man with a crest of wedding-gown-white hair emerges from a cafe in the quiet business district of Clarendon Hills.

His age, easy gait and unassuming demeanor form a perfect image of comfortable suburban retirement.

But the picture quickly changes when the man turns into one of the businesses on Prospect Avenue, climbs behind the president's desk and takes charge handling a slew of clients over the phone.

A retired, 80-year-old man is not supposed to be running a highly successful travel agency that last year tallied more than $1.3 million in sales. But that's exactly what Robert T. Halladay does.

Mr. Halliday retired from Illinois Bell Telephone Co. in 1965 after spending 43 years with the phone company making the long-distance climb from management trainee to division traffic manager for the Loop area. His energy and drive—he still puts in a six-day week—are obvious indications that his main concern at the time was not whether he'd continue working, but where.

Faced with a personal crossroads, Mr. Halladay decided to choose a path he knew and enjoyed—travel. It seems he has a travel bug that can't be exterminated.

"From the very beginning I was interested in traveling. At the University of Chicago, I was involved in athletics (baseball, football and basketball). We got to travel around the country playing other teams, even collegiate basketball in Japan."

In later years, Mr. Halladay and his wife made a pact to keep trying different places. By 1965, they had sojourned to every state in the union, plus Canada, Europe, the Caribbean and the Orient.

Through this vast experience, Mr. Halladay had observed the workings of the travel business. "It occurred to me that although some of the companies that had helped plan our trips were big outfits, I could've done a better job," he says.

A friend in the travel business offered Mr. Halladay a position in his office, but the location was inconvenient. The searcher finally found his oasis when an agency in Clarendon Hills went up for sale.

"It was a very sick agency when I took over," Mr. Halladay remembers, "but my range of acquaintances through the years in business and the community led to a good number of clients. We did a good job. With our background, word got around and people would go out of their way to help us." . . .

Last year's sales constituted a record for the steadily growing Halladay Travel Service Inc. Eight employees now assist him in the office blanketed with brochures and maps. Although planning the trips of amateur Marco Polos provides some enviable fringe benefits, Mr. Halladay is quick to point out that he must deal with all the problems of a big corporation.

But the success of the agency has given Mr. Halliday less to worry about than in its early years. Yet, there are no signs he wants to alleviate that worry completely.

"I've never felt retired," he laughs. "When you get older you're supposed to slow down, but as long as you have the desire to do something, you do it. Maybe everybody isn't that way."

But with the gaze of experience, he disputes that remark. "*Everybody* has to feel they're doing something worthwhile. The agency makes me feel as if I'm doing something important," he says picking up the phone to come quickly to a traveler's aid. "I think that's why I like not being retired. You continue to retain a certain importance."

Seniors' center is the perfect Rx for retired pharmacist

By Sandra Pesmen

There's a sign on the door that says "Se Habla Yiddish."

Inside, a small, very gentle man wearing a natty mauve sport shirt opens his briefcase with a businesslike flourish and takes out a paper titled "Yiddish Discussion Group Agenda."

And 75-year-old David Kaplan—group moderator and retired pharmacist—is ready to begin his busy Tuesday at the Mayer Kaplan Senior Center in Bernard Horwich Center at 3003 W. Touhy.

"I come to the center a couple of days a week," says the druggist who sold his West Side drugstore six years ago. "This group lasts until 11 a.m., then there's a men's talk group where we discuss American heritage and life in general. Later we have lunch, and after that we have a psychology group. Also every Tuesday afternoon Gertrude Bentley, an in-

EXHIBIT 18-2 (Continued)

structor at Truman College, comes to discuss important current events with us. You could be busy here every day."

Except that Mr. Kaplan doesn't have quite that much free time.

The energetic senior, who emigrated from Russia with his parents in 1925, ran a neighborhood drugstore near Madison and Francisco with his pharmacist wife for more than 40 years.

"It was a real riot," he says, making a bad joke. "I mean it—we had plenty of riots there, but every time our store was burned down, we rebuilt because my customers were always fine to me. We had our share of holdups, three or four times a year like clockwork, but we kept coming back for the people. They needed a drugstore."

People still seem to need Mr. Kaplan, but now he fills their orders in a different way.

"Two days a week I deliver Meals on Wheels for the Council of Jewish Elderly because I'm one of them," he says. "But remember, it's not charity—they pay for the food. I never just bring it and run. I go in and meet the people and visit with them."

Other days Mr. Kaplan serves as a *Tolmach*, or interpreter, for newly immigrated Russian Jews looking for jobs and apartments. He serves on the board of the Senior Center, participates in Ezras Israel Congregation, helps Jewish United Fund drives and is past president of Joe Fox Lodge of the B'nai B'rith. He also plays golf.

"When I retired, everybody asked me what I was going to do with myself," he remembers. "But I tell them I don't have enough time to do all the things I like to do."

The thing Mr. Kaplan likes best is serving as *On Ferer*, or moderator, for this Yiddish language group that's now breaking attendance records with up to 60 participants. . . .

Why are these seniors attracted to Mr. Kaplan's group?

"We live in a Christian world and we have Jewish souls," says one.

"Because we're hungry for the sounds of our childhood," says another.

And Mr. Kaplan, always the philosopher, sums it up, "I feel that I'm paying homage to my parents, bringing honor to them, by talking their language and helping others to also."

Giving is what he takes to keep going in retirement

By Bess Gallanis

Gentle Paul Pellegrini likes to say he's a taker. But he isn't. He's a real giver.

Eighty-four-year-old Mr. Pellegrini—who spent most of his working years in the restaurant business with his brothers—went to work as a volunteer at the Shore Training Center for developmentally disabled adults in Skokie nine years ago after retiring for the second time as head chef at the Art Institute.

"I always said when I retired I would work with children, and these kids are great," he says of the handicapped adults who range in age from 17 to 50.

Proudly showing off one of his kids' work, Mr. Pellegrini says, "I set up the shrinking machines that package small toys and trinkets and the young people run them. I compliment them and reward them when they do good work; I bawl them out once in a while."

During his time off, Mr. Pellegrini gathers ceramic tiles from neighborhood stores and draws designs on them. Later, the young people make trivets of them. "After they get the hang of it, I let them make their own designs and express themselves. They do pretty well." . . .

Even though Mr. Pellegrini is not an official counselor, he often takes on counseling responsibilities. "Sometimes the kids get bored doing the same job, like pasting labels on forms, but I talk to them in their language, give them advice about things. Especially the boys—I try to talk to them man-to-man."

The courtly retiree, who is much smaller than most of his charges, also teaches them to do janitorial work. After training, some of his students find work in private industry. "I have one boy who's worked at the Burger King for three years now," he notes with pride.

Although Mr. Pellegrini spends only two days a week at the center—down from three after an accident at Christmas that put him in the hospital for 24 days—he uses his personal time to contribute to the center's clients. "I have a workshop where I make things to bring in for the kids' projects."

He's even taken up political battles for them, fighting everyone from Gov. Thompson to the Reagan administration opposing any form of human resources cutbacks. He wrote form letters and sent them home with the center's clients for their parents to sign, then gathered them up and mailed them in.

This octogenarian claims he'll never get tired of doing this work. "But sometimes I feel guilty. I think that perhaps a younger person just out of school—who's really trained to work with these kids—should be here," he frets. "Yet, the directors keep telling me not to worry about it, so I try not to. They say I'll tell *them* when I'm too old to do this."

He pauses, his hazel eyes become a bit misty as he rationalizes, "I've been asked to teach in a cooking school, but I wouldn't. Not for big money, not for anything. These kids are what keep me going. It's been a very happy thing for me."

Source: *Crain's Chicago Business*, May 25, 1981, pp. 25–27.

EXHIBIT 18-3. Breaking the Rules.

Movin' on: 26-year-old Kenny Brown on the Great American Superhighway

By Steve Yahn

Twenty-six-year-old motorcycle tycoon Kenny Brown is sitting in the dark at R. J. Grunts Restaurant ordering another martini and forgetting about his Evel Knievel shows and his huge motorcycle-mechanics training school and his nationwide motorcycle-repair-and-rental franchises.

Brown is motorcycling his mind out on the Great American Superhighway.

"I used to love to go out on the interstate and get going 80, 90 miles an hour, and then as I was passing a car, lift up my front wheel and do a wheely. It really freaked them out to see you coming by on one wheel. One wheel, man!"

He was the dark, long-haired biker from Chicago. Mary was the beautiful, built blond from Danville, Ill. She was on Greenleaf Beach. He had been dating a rich girl, but she kept him waiting on his cycle in front of one of her father's hotels, so he roared off to the lake, scattering the bleached beach boys lolling around Mary.

BARAPPP! BARAPPP! Don't loll around. Mary didn't. She got on the big, orange Triumph and years later, when he pulled a $13,000 ring out of a pocket in his Levis, they were married and Mary moved into his condominium in Skokie.

"When I was in high school I had what was considered long hair," Brown says. "If you didn't have a crewcut and pegged pants—the college look—people judged you. The guys that were my friends drove motorcycles. If you had long hair and drove a motorcycle, you were really a greaser.

"Some of my friends even quit high school," he says, letting a slight smile slip out.

Strange things that boy was doing. Turning down a scholarship from Francis Parker High School to take machine-shop courses at Lane Tech. Rejecting a General Motors design-school award to work nights on diesel engines at International Harvester. Leaving home at 17. His parents were having trouble. His father was a dentist but didn't want to be. Moving in with a friend's family and opening a bicycle, lawn mower and motorcycle repair shop on Ashland Av.

The first year the wiry, bowlegged kid makes $14,000. Then he buys a Bridgestone motorcycle franchise. Then, at 19, he rents an alley in Old Town for $125 a month and wheels down the first two Bridgestones to what will be . . .

Ken Brown's Cycle World!

Old Town going WILD—300,000 people a weekend jamming the only place where it is—go-go girls, sawdust floors, funky fudge, head shops, big hamburgers, psychedelic posters, boutiques.

And Kenny Brown the only one with wheels on Wells St.!

"I knew motorcycles would go over big," Brown says. "They couldn't miss. Sales were picking up. Honda was doing it with its advertising campaign: 'You meet the nicest people on a Honda.' The image changed from black-leather jackets to meeting the nicest people. I knew there were millions of people who had never ridden who wanted to. We taught them right there. God knows how many people we taught to ride.

"I made it fast. I didn't think there was any end to it. I went out and did crazy things. I bought a Corvette and two Cadillacs and then I got a limousine. I got a big kick out of taking all the mechanics into McDonald's in a chauffeur-driven limousine."

Old Town going WILD! Putting people on motorcycles and letting them ride, 17 hours a day, 7 days a week. Running at night with the Wells St. clan. Drinking at the Crystal Pistol go-go bar. Racing horses at the Dundee dude ranch. Partying all night in his Skokie condominium, not knowing who is staying and not caring, welcoming everybody. And driving off to the gambling casinos in Biloxi, Miss., because somebody whom nobody could remember said the casinos spin and flash and go all night; blasting down hot, steamy-night roads deep into the heart of the country, searching for the neon casinos that never stop.

"Yeah, I miss it," Brown says, ordering another martini in R. J. Grunts. "I miss it because the responsibilities weren't so great. When I first started in Old Town and had only $125-a-month rent in the alley, I was running around in Levis and a T-shirt.

"I was making a lot of money. I had 15 mechanics and 5 salesmen working for me when I was in the garage on Wells, and every night I'd take them out and blow $200 or $300 just on dinner. We went into the Tap Root Pub so much that the guy who owned it named a steak after me—'The KB Double-Steak.' "

High flyin'.

Until the Old Town murders began. And the shootings, knifings and muggings.

"You didn't hear about a lot of the stuff because there was heavy money sunk into the street. But you'd walk a block and maybe get mugged, stabbed, shot. They tried to keep it quiet, but when people were killed, the crowds stopped coming."

So back in 1969, after a petty thief swung a hatchet at his head and almost got it, Kenny Brown said good-by to Old Town.

He moved on, promoting rock concerts and a Mod

EXHIBIT 18-3 (Continued)

Expo Show and "Cycle-Rama" Evel Knievel shows in Chicago and Detroit. But that was a vacation. Soon he was renting a big, blackened-brick warehouse at 2840 N. Halsted St. for. . . .

Ken Brown's American Motorcycle Mechanics Training School!

The first cycle-repair school in Chicago. One of the three biggest in the country.

Kenny Brown going again! Setting up in New Town, working 17 hours a day, training bikers and long-haired dropouts and hundreds of very different dudes wheeling into the warehouse from all over America.

But was somebody saying that from this warehouse Ken Brown is going—nationwide?

Yup, says George Hurstak, a young bony blond who is giving his master's degree in mechanical engineering a regular workout operating one of Brown's Electro-Cycle repair centers at 2036 N. Clark St.

Can't miss, Hurstak says, because of "the machine." The motorcycle-testing machine Brown designed with Sun Electric Corp., the largest automobile-testing equipment maker in the country.

Take two red wires, clamp them to motorcycle spark plugs and, zingo, a whole wall of gauges bleep on and George is rocking and squinting and reading almost any cycle problem in minutes: That's the Electro-Cycle.

Beating olden times by about 150 m.p.h., George says. You can do repairs in 24 hours, not 2 weeks. And the only way you can get one is to buy a franchise.

When Evel Knievel saw the gleaming, gray-metal machine, he believed. In April, Knievel signed a contract to make it the Even Knievel Electro-Cycle performance tester.

Knievel and Brown as partners, Knievel promoting the Electro-Cycle at his shows and signing autographs at grand openings and Ken running the business and improving the machine. He also will keep expanding his AAA Motorcycle Leasing franchises. In Chicago, St. Louis and Florida soon you will be able to lease a motorcycle from Brown like renting a car from Hertz.

Just go into a Spanish-stucco AAA shop, lease a cycle and ride away for three months or six months or whatever. Then when it's time to ride back, if you can't face giving up your machine, well, take those rental payments, throw in some cash or promises and buy the cycle.

R. J. Grunts, in the meantime, is filling up. The place is growing mighty dark.

"Party time at Lori's! Wow! Bring EVERYBODY! I can't wait!"

Lori the dark-haired waitress talking up her Friday night party, shimmering right there in front of Brown in her watery-red blouse and tight blue jeans.

He looks at her with his big brown Omar Shariff eyes (older movie fans say Erroll Flynn), but he doesn't say anything.

"Now LOOK, man," Lori says, "I really want you to come to my party. Bring whatever it takes to get you off."

And Lori is off, inviting EVERYBODY to come to her party.

"Sure I've had some business failures," says Brown, who is pushing past his first million dollars.

Like New Year's two years ago when he threw a three-day Mod Expo Show at the Amphitheatre and the hassles stacked up to heaven.

"They thought every hippie in the country was going to show up and smoke dope. We heard that word came down from the mayor not to let it go. They closed the doors early, they screwed up traffic, they did everything.

"I lost my shirt—$70,000.

"Some people really thrive on you being down. The stories that get back—if I have a problem in business, or make an investment in something and lose a chunk of money, some people think it's the greatest thing. And these guys are supposed to be my friends. We grew up together. It's unbelievable the way people are about money.

"Sometimes I think about giving it all up and building my ranch in Arizona, but then I wonder if I wouldn't be missing something."

He would be missing hustling 20 hours a day during the "Cycle-Rama" production, losing 20 pounds in two weeks making sure the Amphitheatre is full when Knievel kicks on his motorcycle and jumps 13, 14, 15 cars—or kills himself.

And he would be missing driving up to Lori's party in his shiny black limousine, stepping out into the damp and drizzle and following the noise in the night on W. Belmont St.

Ken and Mary crowding up the old, dark stairway with hundreds of people off the New Town streets; Kenny Brown jamming into Lori's party, dark eyes flashing, in there doing it, keeping it going.

Moving on. . . .

Source: *Done in a Day*, pp. 325–29. © Field Enterprises, Inc.

EXERCISE 18-1

Try a feature story on a collection of people who do "dirty jobs" that nobody else wants to do and yet get lots of flak from the public for their efforts. These can include the baseball umpire in your town, the IRS man who has to call and tell you he wants to see you because there's something wrong with the return you filed, or the person in the department store in charge of complaints.

Interview three of them—or others that you think of yourself. Ask:

- What do you do? Please describe it.

- When you deal with the public, do people laugh at you—or yell?

- How do you feel about their response, and how can you keep on doing the job?

- Why do you stay on the job? Is there some redeeming feature in it that I can't see?

- What's the best experience you've had doing this work?

- What's the worst—the one that made you think you'd have to quit?

- Do you feel you're performing a service to mankind that justifies the frustration?

- What's your secret fantasy about work—what dream job would you really like to do—or is this it?

- Tell me about your home life and hobbies. Are they different from your job?

- Do you have any interesting stories about your daily work?

Write a short story about each person, 400 words each.

EXERCISE 18-2

Why do you think Yahn's story worked so well? What are the tensions and contrasts that you see in Kenny Brown's life? Can you see how much time Yahn spent filling his pack with information? Where do you suppose he did his interviews? What devices in the story tell you the most about the subject?

How else might the story have been handled?

Conclusion

There's one more ingredient vital to producing good writing of any kind—self-confidence.

In order for any creative activity to begin, the creator must have good feelings about himself, and sometimes that's difficult in an editorial setting.

For instance: Your account executive tosses your press kit back on your desk and says, "You missed the point and you're too wordy. The lead is on page two. Rewrite the story by 4:00 P.M. today."

And you block.

You begin thinking, "I'm stupid. If I was a good writer, I'd have done it right the first time. He doesn't like my work. He doesn't like me. Why can't I do things right, right away? If he really liked having me on his staff he wouldn't discourage me this way."

You are thinking negative thoughts, and most of them are wrong.

If you had confidence in yourself and your skills, you'd think, "He's right. I'm really lucky to have a good editor who can spot the lead. It's nice of him to share his knowledge with me. It's easy to cut out the redundant words once someone who's more experienced than I am has pointed them out. And isn't it great that my boss thinks so much of me, he's willing to take the time to go over my work so carefully? He must really want me to perform well as a member of his team."

Certainly that's a more rational, positive view, but you can't think that way unless you feel positively about yourself.

Here are some tips for doing that.

Dr. David D. Burns, psychiatrist at the University of Pennsylvania Medical School's Mood Clinic, is one of the prime developers of the new Cognitive Therapy program that helps depressed, stressful, and anxious people feel good about themselves. He describes the program in the best-seller *Feeling Good.*

He defines distorted thought patterns as:

1. *All or nothing thinking.* You see things in black and white categories. If your performance falls short of perfect, you see yourself as a total failure.
2. *Overgeneralization.* You see a single negative as a never-ending pattern of defeat.
3. *Using a mental filter.* You pick out a single negative detail and dwell on it exclusively, so your vision of all reality becomes darkened, like a drop of ink that discolors an entire beaker of water.
4. *Disqualifying the positive.* You reject positive experiences by insisting they "don't count" for some reason. In this way you can maintain a negative belief that's contradicted by your positive everyday experiences.
5. *Jumping to conclusions.* You make a

negative interpretation, even though there are no definite facts that support your conclusion.

6. *Magnification.* You exaggerate the importance of things (such as a goof-up) or shrink things (if they are your own desirable qualities).

7. *Emotional reasoning.* You assume your negative emotions reflect things accurately.

8. *Making "should" statements.* You try to motivate yourself with "shoulds" and "shouldn'ts," as if you had to be whipped and punished before you could be expected to do anything. "Musts" and "oughts" are also offenders. All produce guilt.

9. *Personalization.* You see yourself as the cause of a negative external event when, in fact, you were not primarily responsible for it.

Obviously, just reading the list once won't solve the problem. But if negative thoughts are flooding your mind and causing self-defeating emotions and you at least realize it, you will begin to set yourself free.

And, once you do that, you'll find yourself turning to the typewriter with confidence and joy. Your ideas will flow freely, words will link together beautifully, and you'll begin to think about how lucky you are to be able to get up in the morning and run to your job—where you have the opportunity to write.